The Ultimate Investing Strategies Collection for Beginners

Proven Strategies to Make Money Investing in Stocks, Real Estate and Cryptocurrencies

By Mark Swing

The following Book is reproduced below with the goal of providing information that is as accurate and reliable as possible. Regardless, purchasing this Book can be seen as consent to the fact that both the publisher and the author of this book are in no way experts on the topics discussed within and that any recommendations or suggestions that are made herein are for entertainment purposes only. Professionals should be consulted as needed prior to undertaking any of the action endorsed herein.

This declaration is deemed fair and valid by both the American Bar Association and the Committee of Publishers Association and is legally binding throughout the United States.

Furthermore, the transmission, duplication, or reproduction of any of the following work including specific information will be considered an illegal act irrespective of if it is done electronically or in print. This extends to creating a secondary or tertiary copy of the work or a recorded copy and is only allowed with the express written consent from the Publisher. All additional right reserved.

The information in the following pages is broadly considered a truthful and accurate account of facts and as such, any inattention, use, or misuse of the information in question by the reader will render any resulting actions solely under their purview. There are no scenarios in which the publisher or the original author of this work can be in any fashion deemed liable for any hardship or damages that may befall them after undertaking information described herein.

Additionally, the information in the following pages is intended only for informational purposes and should thus be thought of as universal. As befitting its nature, it is presented without assurance regarding its prolonged validity or interim quality. Trademarks that are mentioned are done without written consent and can in no way be considered an endorsement from the trademark holder.

Table of Contents

Introduction

Congratulations on purchasing this book, and thank you for doing so. The world of investing is growing increasingly chaotic. Getting this book is the first step that you can take towards doing something about your financial situation. The first step will not always be the easiest, which is why the information you will find in the following chapters is so important to take to heart, as they are not concepts that can be put into action immediately. If you file these concepts away for when you need them, when the time comes to use them, you will be glad you have them at hand.

The following chapters will discuss the primary preparedness principles that you will need to consider if you ever hope to make money investing.

I am happy to welcome you to the world of investing and to help you make more money.

Chapter 1

Why You Must Stave First and Then Invest

Very often the concepts of saving and investing are confused, as well as that of "saver" and "investor." However, there are substantial differences that need to be understood, before diving deeper into the subject of money.

In this first chapter, we will explain what saving and investing are, analyzing which choice is more convenient today.

Saving means taking out a portion of income received, that you deliberately choose not to consume immediately, but to store in a bank account for the future. Saving often results in the tranquillity guaranteed by the availability of resources to deal with unexpected situations.

Savings can then be allocated to investment, and this is the main analogy between the two concepts. The investment may be of the "economic" type (such as the purchase of a car or company machinery), or of the "financial" type (such as the purchase of a security or mutual fund with the objective to see capital growth over time). However, unlike savings, in the case of investing, the achievement of the desired objective is not certain (for example, a stock may lose value), so the result can be negative, compromising the amounts saved.

Which is better?
If the question that arises is whether it is better to save or invest, the answer is probably "both." The choice depends on your financial situation and your personal goals.

Savings can be used to invest, but can also be used in other ways. In fact, the money saved can also be deposited in the bank to reduce risks (theft). But this, unlike what many think, is a wrong and unprofitable choice: money, in fact, tends to lose purchasing power over time due to inflation. In other words, if you save 100 Dollars today, in 20 years, you will be able to get less out of that money than today. This is why saving money is, often, the wrong choice if you want to get wealthy.

Assuming an average increase in the cost of living around 2% and a saved sum of 5,000 Dollars, in five years this sum will fall to real 4,500 Dollars, that is 10% less (excluding banking taxes!). Obviously, you can keep the savings at home (under the classic mattress!), But with all the risks that come with it.

What is the difference between investing and saving? Let's repeat it once again to get it better. Saving means putting money aside little by little in order to accumulate a certain sum. Usually, you save for a certain goal, like going on vacation, buying a car or for emergencies that could happen.

Instead, investing means taking a part of the money to make it grow, buying tools that can increase its value like shares, houses, funds or ETFs.

Who should save?

Obviously, everyone should try to save a part of their money. The rule is to have away on your bank account at least the necessary to "survive" for three months and cover the main expenses (such as food and rent). This will offer air pocket, in case of inconvenient and unexpected situations.

Saving is, therefore, a rule and as every good rule has its exceptions. You can, in fact, stop putting aside the money when:

1. you have too much debt, and you are trying to pay it off;
2. the family has priority and could not go on in case of unfortunate events to one of its members.

Even when you have set aside enough for emergencies, you do not have to stop saving. The goal of everyone should be to put aside at least 10% of their salary every month, perhaps starting from 5% and gradually scaling up. To make things easier, you can save money by thinking of any objective, like having enough money for a great honeymoon or to get a new car.

Having a goal is essential, so you know what you're saving for. Every reach person has financial goals, so it is a good habit to pick up.

When is the time to invest?
Like when you save money, you need to have a goal to when and how to invest your savings. In this case, it is important to know what your short, medium and long-term goals are.

- With "short term" we mean goals for the next three years;
- With "medium term," things are planned for the next 3-10 years
- The "long-term" goals are those for which you will not need the money back for at least ten years or more

For short-term objectives, you usually invest through deposit accounts, which allow you to get a minimum return in a short amount of time. However, this has been a bit shrinking in the last period (deposit rates are at the lowest). For the medium-long term objectives, it is instead advisable to invest in the market, to avoid the reduction in value that inflation produces on "still" money. The market usually guarantees higher returns than deposit accounts over longer periods and having a well-constructed portfolio helps a lot in this regard.

For those approaching or exceeding 30 years of age, having a medium-long term goal is advisable. Investing and setting aside money for retirement can be a good start.

To sum up the concept, everything depends on your time horizon:

- If you think about using the money within one or three years, save it.

- If you do not need this money for the next ten years, invest it.

If, on the other hand, you plan on using the savings in the next 5 or 10 years, but you want to still have money set aside in your bank account, then you will have to do both. Keep in mind that this is much harder and requires more discipline. However, with the right mindset, it is certainly the best option.

What does investing wisely mean?
Since the importance of the investment is well established, it should also be emphasized that there is no recipe to guarantee the success of an investment.

However, following some prudential rules can help minimize risks.

First of all, we need to avoid the dream of making money overnight. On the market, there are professional operators, experts, who dedicate all their time to this activity, but they often make mistakes as well. Just to say how difficult it is and how "get rich quick schemes" do not exist.

One strategy that every investor needs to master to reduce the risk is diversification. This means not putting all your eggs in one basket, but spreading your resources on different assets. When the invested amount grows it becomes more important to diversify not only between the asset classes (stocks, bonds, commodities) but also geographically (taking into account the currency variable) and size-wise (small or big cap companies to stay within the equity, more or less long maturities for government securities, bonds with different level of risk in the corporate sphere).

Making these choices takes time, that needs to be subtracted from work or other activities. So, in the end, it is about investing time, before moving the money. But it is worth it and, frankly speaking, the only option to avoid reckless choices that you may regret afterward.

Let's not hide behind the common opinion that you do not have money to invest. Do not get us wrong; you may be in the situation where money is tight, and you do not have the resources to make a decisive move in the market. However, you can always control your cash flow and add extra streams of income. These will provide you with more money, that you need to save for future investments. We know it is hard, but it is possible, and most millionaires started with nothing.

To us, mindset is extremely valuable, and in this chapter, we want to debunk once and for all the most recurring excuses people use to avoid or postpone their investments.

1. "I do not have time to invest."

One of the most common excuses is to believe that investing can take away most of the precious time we have available. The truth is that we are committing a big error of assessment. Investing does not require a specific amount of time: you can choose how much time you want to dedicate to it. Obviously, the more, the better, but you can even start with a few minutes a day.

Thanks to the advent of the internet and new technologies, in fact, investing is now just a click away, thus reducing not only the costs of negotiation but also the time required.

2. "I do not have enough money to invest."

To believe that investing is a subject reserved for those with large quantities of money is one of the worst mistakes we can make. Let's dispel this myth immediately: it is not true that to make money we need big money. There are affordable financial products that do not require the fortunes of Scrooge McDuck to start planning your future.

From today it is possible to start saving and investing starting from just 5 euros.

Think about it, 5 euros equals five coffees a week. If we had saved a coffee a day for five days a week since the euros came into force, until the end of 2016, we would have put aside a "small" sum of €3865. If these savings, instead of being forgotten in our piggy bank, were invested in global equity markets, at the end of 2016 we would have had €7493. No savings are therefore insignificant to be invested.

3. "I do not have the skills to invest."

One of the reasons that drive us away from investing is to convince ourselves that we do not have the right skills and knowledge. Investing in financial markets may seem difficult, but the truth is that you do not have to be Warren Buffett to start doing it. By investing in mutual funds, for example, our savings are entrusted to a team of expert managers who make the investment choices for us on a daily basis. While we let others manage our money, it is fundamental to learn. Remember that the goal is to become an investor that takes care of his resources.

4. "I will invest in a few years when I have a higher salary."

Delaying an investment is not a wise choice, especially considering the benefits of compound interest capitalization. To show you, we have compared two capital accumulation plans: the first invests a sum of € 100 a month from the age of 25, while the second invests € 200 a month but starts from 35 years.

In your opinion, which of the two would be able to obtain a higher capital at the age of 70?

The accumulation plan of 100 € monthly, undertaken for 25 years, will have generated at the age of 70 a capital of 520,000 euros: 50,000 more than the other.

Anticipating the investment, not only requires less economic effort but also allows you to obtain higher earnings compared to a higher investment delayed over time.

5. "Investing is too risky."

None of us wants to lose money, but we do not realize that we are already doing this when we decide not to invest. If the alternative to investing is, in fact, to feel safe by parking our savings on the bank account, inflation could reserve us unpleasant surprises reducing inexorably our purchasing power in the future.

If you invest using portfolio diversification and adopting a long-term time horizon, the chances of losing money are reduced a lot.

Chapter 2

Investing in The Stock Market

Most beginners investors and traders have quite confused ideas when approaching the stock market, investing in stocks (or options, ETFs), commodities, etc.) or trading in general.

One of the pivotal points that creates confusion in the mind of those interested in making their money work through investments is the lack of understanding of the crucial difference that exists between trading and investing.

The confusion derives from the fact that in the eyes of the investor or the uneducated and non-conscious trader, doing trading or investing seems to be the same thing.

In reality, although they are united by the desire to make a profit, the two operations arise from different logics and follow different rules.

In fact, those who invest in a measure of the value of what they buy (an action, a house, a business, an object of art, etc.), try to buy it at a discounted or otherwise balanced price, and the entire operation is based on the prediction or hope that, over time, the good purchased will increase in value and that this increase in value will automatically be reflected in a corresponding increase in its market price allowing it to be sold for a profit.

An easily understandable example of investment is that of those who buy agricultural land in the expectation that it will then be buildable.

The greatest investors of history, such as the legendary Warren Buffett, are in fact masters in buying "depreciated quality." Of course, their time horizon is never very short, and the value of what they have purchased can remain or even go down for a certain period without this causing them to worry excessively.

Who trades, however, does not bet on a change in the value of things. To be honest, the hard and pure trader does not care highly about the objective quality or the nature of what he buys, he is only interested in acquiring it at a price that (in a generally rather short time frame) he plans to grow, regardless of the fact that the value of what he purchased remains perfectly identical.

In fact, what makes trading possible is simply the fact that the prices of things (and therefore also investment objects such as shares, bonds, real estate, etc.) may vary regardless of their value due to the law of the application and the offer.

An example out of context of activity comparable to trading is that of the Super Bowl tickets reseller, who obtains the tickets three weeks earlier at regular prices and then resells them at the last moment when lacking tickets and many questions, he can market them to a much higher price.

On an exchange, for an investor, it is crucial to understand what he is buying and what the current and future value of the company he is planning to buy shares is. In other words, investors search quality companies that are currently depreciated.

On the other hand, for a trader, it is sufficient to use tools (generally the stock's graph evaluated through technical analysis) that allow him to make a forecast of the future price of the stock regardless of the value of the company and its corporate purpose.

The stock market is a great place to invest your money in. Here are a few tips to be successful at it.

- *"If you are undecided, stay still."* It is not necessary to invest continuously. If you do not have precise ideas, it is better to do nothing and wait for clearer signs. Often, the market is full of indecision: keep calm and stack up money for the future.

- *"Cut losses and let profits run."* This is perhaps the best known and most important rule for those investing in the stock market. An indispensable factor for the application of this rule is the identification, immediately after the purchase, of the stop loss. This is how much you are willing to lose on that investment (take into account when determining the average daily excursion of the stock). The cold and systematic application, even if painful, of the stop loss will preserve you from huge losses that would make the sale more and more traumatic, freezing capital that could be invested elsewhere.

- *"Learn from your mistakes."* Errors are not always negative: if you follow a strategy with a method, if you apply the stop losses, you will not make particularly serious mistakes. Errors are an integral part of stock trading: you need to analyze why you made them and what you can learn from them. In this way, a small loss can become a good investment lesson for the future.

- *"Take profit and invest them back."* If one of our titles is on the rise, take profit will be applied as the stock grows. A stock cannot grow indefinitely, when the trend is reversed, selling at the top, we will have had a profit avoiding further descents. If then the title should go up again, it does not matter; it will go better next time. You can not always sell at the top since remember, you cannot time the market.

- *"Buy on the rumor and sell on the news."* When positive news on a certain title officially come out, pay attention. It may already be too late to invest in that title since the market could already have priced it in.

- *Do not believe in "safe investments."* If someone tells you that a title will certainly reach a certain price, he either does not understand much of the stock market or is only doing his interests.

- *"Never become emotionally attached to a stock."* Some investors always follow a limited number of companies that they consider more reliable than others. There are no titles better than others, but only favorable situations and unfavorable situations. Often, instead of admitting an error, one perseveres on it with the consequence of being heavily unbalanced on a stock. This is bad, especially if you are overcommitted to a stock in which, at that moment, the market does not believe in.

- *"Always maintain a certain liquidity available."* Cyclically we find ourselves in situations of several days of generalized decline of the whole stock exchange and often, for lack of liquidity, we can not grasp excellent buying opportunities. Keep some money aside to jump on big opportunities.

- *"Choose the right platform."* One important rule for investing in the stock market is that the platform makes the difference. Carefully selecting safe, honest and reliable trading platforms is the first step to make money. Those who start investing in the stock market for the first time must be careful to choose platforms that are simple to use, perhaps with high-quality educational support. Some platforms also offer add-on tools, such as notifications, social trading, and free analysis tools, to guide less experienced traders.

- *"Invest only in what you understand."* As the "guru" of finance, Warren Buffett said, "never, never, invest in something that you do not understand, and above all, that you do not know." The overwhelming majority of investors can achieve their capital growth goals by using the most common financial instruments, which are almost always simple to understand. The complex tools are best left to the great experts in the field.

- *"Diversify your portfolio."* When investing, the word to keep in mind is "diversification." Never invest in a single title, because if that sinks, your money will come to the same end. It is always better to have diversified investments to minimize the specific risks of a company, a market, an asset class or a currency. The more you diversify and the lower the probability of having drastic falls.

- *"Understand and evaluate the risk."* Risk is an intrinsic component of every investment. If it does not exist, there is no return. Whether they are government bonds, stocks or mutual funds, they all have a risk component, which will obviously be greater if you want to hope for higher returns. So, if someone tells you that there is an investment without risk, it means that it is better to get advice from someone else.

- *"Look beyond direct investment."* As an alternative to direct purchase of shares, it is possible to invest in the stock market indexes, through ETFs (listed mutual funds, which replicate the performance of equity and bond indices), or in mutual funds, that offer a high diversification even with minimum amounts, allow you to invest small periodic shares, for example, 100 euros per month, and may even provide a monthly coupon.

- *"Do not follow the masses."* The typical decision of who buys stocks by investing in the stock market is usually strongly influenced by the advice of acquaintances, neighbors or relatives. So, if everyone around is investing in a particular company, a beginner investor tends to do the same. But this strategy is bound to fail in the long run, and it is not the right approach. There should be no need to say that you should always avoid having a herd mentality if you do not want to lose hard-earned money on the stock market. The world's biggest investor, Warren Buffett, is right when he says "Be fearful when others are greedy, and be greedy when others are fearful!"

- *"Do not try to time the market."* One thing that Warren Buffett does not do is try to time the stock market, even if he has a very strong understanding of the key price levels of the single shares. Most investors, however, do exactly the opposite, which often causes losses of money. So, you should never try to give timing the market a chance. In reality, no one has ever succeeded in doing so successfully and consistently over multiple market cycles.

- *"Be disciplined."* Historically, it has often happened that during periods of a high market upswing, we first caused moments of panic.

Market volatility has inevitably made investors poorer, even if the market moved in the intended direction. Therefore, it is prudent to have patience and follow a disciplined investment approach as well as keeping a long-term general picture in mind.

- *"Be realistic and do not hope."* There is nothing wrong with hoping to make the best investment, but you could be in trouble if the financial goals are not based on realistic assumptions. For example, many stocks have generated more than 50 percent of returns during the big uptrend in recent years. However, this does not mean that we can always expect the same kind of return from the stock exchange.

- *"Keep your portfolio under control."* We live in a connected world. Every important event that happens anywhere in the world also has an impact on our money. So, we have to constantly monitor our portfolio and make adjustments.

- *"Be sure to be on the legal side of things."* If someone proposes an investment, it must be verified as an "authorized project." In our country, those who offer financial investments must be authorized by law, and this is an important safeguard for savers. In fact, the authorization is issued only in the presence of the requested requisites and, once authorized, the financial intermediaries are subject to constant supervision. Checking this is not particularly demanding: if you have internet you can even directly access the information held by the supervisory authorities; otherwise you can contact the authorities themselves using traditional means.

- *"Be skeptical and do your research."* Nobody gives anything for nothing: be wary of investment proposals that ensure a very high return. At the promise of high returns, there are usually very high risks or, in some cases, even attempts of fraud. Be wary of "Ponzi schemes" which promise profits linked to the subsequent adhesion of other subjects, who often must be convinced by the investor himself to join. These "operations," in fact, can not guarantee any return, as they are normally supplied exclusively by the continuity of the accessions. In other words, when the new signatures are no longer sufficient to pay the "interests" to the previous subscribers, the schemes are destined to fail. Be wary of the vague and generic investment proposals, for which the methods for using the money collected are not explained in detail (what kind of securities will be purchased, at what prices, on which markets, with which risk profiles - interest rate, foreign exchange or counterparty - and whether and which hedging instruments will be used to cover such risks).

- *"Have a long-term mindset."* According to Warren Buffett, the shares once bought, are not to be sold. It is, therefore, better to evaluate the industrial trends in the long term and then buy them, leaving aside the passengers' enthusiasm.

- *"When investing in real estate, know the area*

you are investing in." To start with, it is good that you put your focus on your area of residence or, if you live in a big city, even in your neighborhood or on one that you know well. If you think to act on a field of action too large, you risk dispersing too much energy towards something that can present different solutions. Dedicate yourself only to residential buildings, apartments or houses. The commercial ones, even if they can be very profitable, have other rules and in general greater difficulties. The same for the land: you can do big business, but it is not something suitable for those who start.

- *"Choose the right leverage and use it to your advantage."* Real estate investments must be made with leverage. If you want to invest only with your money, then the essence of real estate investment is not clear to you. In fact, the concept of financial leverage allows you to invest with money that is not yours but to make money directly for you. Leverage an economic tool that allows you to get where you would not get only with your strength. You can take out a mortgage (if you can afford it) or engage financial partners. It may seem strange to you but it is not at all: even the richest need partners and remember that a figure that seems almost unimaginable to you, it may be normal to somebody else.

- *"Verba volant, scripta manent"* the Latins used to say. So never make verbal agreements, even if it is a relative or a childhood friend. Consult a lawyer to have the templates of the documents to be used. Like everything, at first it will seem difficult, but after a few times you will become an expert in basic legal practices for the sale of real estate, and you will be able to create documents in a very short time even by yourself.

- *"Consider shorter positions."* In the fixed income universe, a short duration approach is potentially able to reduce sensitivity to rising interest rates, while optimizing the returns/risk ratios.

- *"Know your risk/reward ratio."* A higher return may be tempting, but you must be sure not to take too many risks about the remuneration you would get. In bond markets, this means avoiding lengthening duration in a context of rising interest rates. Increasing investments in riskier assets may seem appropriate at the moment when the macroeconomic scenario is quite positive, but it could turn out to be a rather risky choice if the situation should change. For example, the yields offered by high yield debt, on average 3% in Europe and 5.5% in the United States, would not be sufficient to compensate investors if insolvencies passed from their current level of 2% to a more normal one of the 5%. Conversely, market areas with a good risk/return profile, with high-rated issuers offering attractive returns, include emerging market debt, subordinated financial bonds, and hybrid corporate bonds. Aiming at long-term quality makes it possible to take on fair risks, helping to limit the impact of any negative macroeconomic event.

- *"Take the currency pairing into account."* Global investments expose to currency risks. High yield bonds and emerging market funds, for example, are usually denominated in US dollars, but the underlying bonds they hold may be issued in another currency. Fund managers may choose to include currency risk in the overall portfolio risk as exchange rates fluctuate, or decide to contain this risk through currency hedging.

- *"Stay flexible, keep some cash aside."* It is important to have the flexibility to underwrite and liquidate investments to seize the best opportunities. However, trades are expensive and can quickly erode earnings. This happens above all in the bond markets, given the relatively low levels of returns. The bid-ask spread is on average 30-40% of the yield, so an excess of trades erodes this margin and obviously reduces the total return. Even holding portfolios with structurally short duration, allowing short-term bonds to come to maturity naturally, can improve returns because you will effectively pay the bid-ask spread once.

- *"Build up your portfolio over time."* If investing a small sum such as 5000 Euro, will not allow you to live on that income, it can certainly represent an opportunity, to make money. In addition, even if you have good economic availability, the ideal is always "to take it safe," starting investing from small figures and then fuel the investment over time.

- *"The past does not equal the future."* The story is not indicative of how an investment will result in the future and investors should always try to weigh the potential risks associated with a particular investment, as well as its possible returns.

Since this is a guide for beginners and most people that start out decide to begin their investing journey with stocks, we thought it would be interesting to lay out the foundation of the topic. For those who choose to invest in stocks, the objective is undoubtedly that of obtaining the highest possible remuneration from their investment, which is why the choice of securities on which to invest their money is of fundamental importance.

Invest in stocks

In this regard, there are no universally valid and reliable rules that allow you to obtain good earnings and eliminate risks of losses; otherwise, the number of investors would be much higher.

In other words, the safe stocks to invest in, if they had ever existed in the past, today are officially extinct! However, this does not mean that plans cannot be made to reduce risk while maintaining a high level of profit. Those who choose to invest in shares today are perfectly aware that there are some parameters that experts believe are essential to take into account when identifying the shares to be included in an investment portfolio. These parameters are the capitalization of the company, the profitability of equity, the ratio between profit and price, the ratio of Ratio to price book value, the dividend yield and the ratings/target price. Let's see what these individual parameters consist of in detail, and how we can use them to choose the stocks to invest in today.

- *Capitalization of companies*: although this is a very often underestimated parameter, we must nevertheless consider that the size of the company is very often a sign of market power, in most cases through the possession of brands or technologies exploited globally. The use of this parameter, however, makes sense especially for equity investments in the US market, where over the last year companies with high capitalization (Apple, Coca-Cola, Facebook, Google, Amazon, etc.) have seen a significant performance. The close relationship existing in the US shareholding between the level of capitalization on the stock exchange and the performance of the stock is one of the factors underlying the growing weight that American stocks have in the portfolios of international investors. The interest of traders in US stocks has also increased in light of the boom in listed companies operating in the tech and web segment.

- *Return over equity (Roe)*: this is the ratio between the net result and the net assets of a given company. In particular from the point of view of equity investments is an important parameter as a profitability higher than the cost of capital is an index of the ability of an enterprise to create value. From this point of view, the Roe is always held in strong consideration by those who choose to invest in shares today.

- *Price/earnings ratio*: a low ratio of this parameter makes a share price particularly attractive, but at the same time it could mean that expectations regarding future profits are not particularly positive. As in the case of the Roe, this is a factor to be taken into consideration when choosing the best stocks to invest in.

- *Price/value ratio*: the ratio between the share price and the net asset value resulting from the last balance sheet, especially if this ratio is lower than the unit means that the company is being paid less than the value of the budget net of liabilities. However, this does not necessarily mean that it is a good deal, since the company may not be able to produce profits either.

- *Dividend yield*: this is the percentage ratio between the last distributed dividend and the share price, in particular, it measures the remuneration provided by the company to shareholders in the last year in the form of liquidity. This parameter is often taken into account to identify the stocks to invest in, since a company able to distribute dividends is generally a healthy company, but also in this case, as with all the other selection parameters, it is necessary to make a broader and more complete analysis, since a high level of this indicator could also mean that the company has made few investments or has little prospect of growth. For this reason, looking at the dividend yield as a primary factor in determining the securities on which to invest in the stock market is reductive. The dividend yield only makes sense if accompanied by considerations on any business plans and industrial plans of the listed company. Only in this way is it possible to have guarantees on what are the prospects of the group in the future.

- *Rating and target price*: the rating is the judgment that certain analysts and investment banks have on a specific listed security while the target price represents the maximum target price to which the shares may reach. Dozens of judgments are published daily on all listed shares. Giving an eye to these judgments is a way to have further clarification on what may be the prospects of the listed. If, in fact, more brokers decide to cut the rating on an X stock from buy to neutral or worse sell, then it means that, indeed, the expectations of the security in question are certainly not positive and therefore, perhaps, it is not the case to insert this title in the list of shares to invest in.

Clearly, promotions and failures (upgrades and downgrades) are not in the air but are accompanied by reports within which are explained the reasons behind that single judgment. Therefore, rating and target price are one of the most important factors for choosing the best stocks to invest in. As the great traders who focus on equities perfectly know, by looking at the history or the evolution of the rating and target price of a single stock, one can have an even more complete picture in the choice of actions to invest in today.

These are the main indicators that will dictate whether your investment will be successful or not. Taking time to study the structure of the company you want to invest in is extremely important since it gives you the opportunity to get a better idea of where it is going and what it is aiming at for the future. Remember that when you invest in stocks, you own part of that project: it is your duty to understand it fully.

Chapter 3

Unusual Steps Internet Marketers Forget

Have you ever heard of the 80/20 rule? Sometimes they call it the principle of the scarcity of factors, and it was originally called the Pareto Principle. It was born at the beginning of the 20th century when Vilfredo Pareto discovered that in Italy 80 percent of the land was owned by 20 percent of the population.

Fast forward a few years, we realized how the rule could be applied in the business world. In most cases, 20 percent of the customers represent the vast majority, or 80 percent, of their turnover. And today the 80/20 rule lends itself to any interesting interpretation.

To take advantage of the 80/20 rule within your company, you focus on 20 percent of the best customers, which guarantee you 80 percent of your sales.

To take advantage of the 80/20 rule to manage your time you focus on 20 percent of the things you do, the ones that matter to you or your business. In other words, the highest value activities (also called "high money value activities").

Pareto's law is dramatically effective when applied to sales and marketing situations. However, the use of Pareto's theory in sales and marketing is generally neglected completely.

The Pareto rule at the simple level suggests that, if there are two groups of data typically related to cause and effect, or input and output, the correlation measured by the data of reality is that:

- "80 percent of the output is produced by 20 percent of the inputs."
- "80 percent of the results are given by 20

percent of the causes."

- "20% of the nature of the costs generates 80% in absolute value of the costs."
- "20% of customers generate 80% of revenues."
- "20% of products generate 80% of revenues."
- "20% of non-compliance causes 80% of non-compliance

You can apply this relationship to any variable. The Pareto principle is an extremely useful model or theory, with infinite applications. Often the optimal ratio regarding identifying the minimum percentage that will produce the best improvement is closer to 90:10 or even 99: 1.

The numbers in their ratio must not necessarily reach 100. The two numbers in an optimal ratio can have more than 100 or less than 100.

For example, there may be a situation where 99% of the result is produced by 15% of the factors or when 75% of the results are derived from 5% of the factors.

So even if a situation contains an 80:20 correlation,

other relationships may be more significant, for example:

- 99:22 (which demonstrates an even greater concentration of 80:20)
- 5:50 (i.e. 5% of the results comes from 50% of inputs or causes) which means a huge amount of activities with ineffective content).

The reasons that allowed the 80:20 ratio to become the "standard" relationship is that on large numbers it remains the most surprising and commonly found relationship in reality.

Remember, for any particular situation the precise ratio can and will probably be different from 80:20, but the principle still applies, and in many cases, the actual ratio will not be far from the general rule of 80:20.

This principle is extremely useful for planning, analyzing and solving problems and achieving goals.

Many disasters in the business could have been easily avoided with a consistent approach of the Pareto Principle. It is a tremendously powerful model, and it is so powerful because it is so simple and easy.

For example, consider an organization that continues to run its business across its product range, when perhaps 95% of its profits come from just 10% of the products and/or perhaps only 2% of its profits comes from 60%, the same concerning customers.

Imagine the wasted effort. Instead, by making a quick analysis of "Pareto's rule" by discovering this reality, decision-makers can see where to direct their efforts, and probably reduce a lot of bad products and better focus on customers and products that are more profitable.

This is something most internet marketers forget, and it is extremely valuable for long-term success.

Chapter 4

Investing in Your Business

Another great way to invest your money is to invest it in a business. Here are some ways you can do that.

Let's see what the main ways to create a passive and automatic monthly online income are:

1. Sell one or more services, automating the process as much as possible.
2. Sell content, in the form of books, ebooks, courses or info-products.
3. Selling through others, earning from affiliation.
4. Monetize content published in other ways (e.g. with advertising space)

At the moment I (like many others here in America and the rest of the world) earn from all four sources. Naturally, each of these ways of creating passive income presupposes the initial work and, in many cases, also the subsequent work although sporadic to maintain the vitality of the source of income. As you have noticed, in fact, in all three cases we talk about "selling", which presupposes that there are buyers and that there is a need to reach them by letting them know in some way (possibly without investing in advertising), and at the same time that there is a "product" to sell to these people, something that may interest them for any reason.

We will try to examine these four ways one by one so that you can understand which one is the best one for you, that is, with which you feel more affinity about your interests, your passions, and your abilities.

1. Passive income from the sale of services or online applications

This is one of the most effective methods to create an automated passive online income, but unlike the other three methods presented below it requires a small investment to register a suitable domain and Web space, as well as greater technical expertise.

For this type of passive income, in fact, we consider services such as ad sites or those that allow you to manage technical aspects of activity on the Web, proposed in the freemium formula, or with a free basic version that involves limitations of use and a more complete paid version where the limitations are 'unlocked'.

In the first category there are, for example, sites where people can post ads of various kinds made with themes or dedicated plugins (using CMS as WordPress), such as those for the sale of used equipment or to meet other people (ad sites) or online dating, or tourist portals that give visibility to advertisers and earn every time they sell their service (it is the case of the hospitality industry with sites like TripAdvisor, Wimdu, etc.), or other sites that put freelancers with potential customers in connection, and so on.

In the second category, on the other hand, there may be included sites that manage, for example, the backup of a site or its maintenance, facilitate networking or collaborative activities of a professional nature, and so on. It goes without saying that it is not enough to develop and put online this type of services, but that we must then promote them both initially and periodically so that more and more people are registered, and naturally we must manage them with an equally regular maintenance to avoid problems of stability or security on the site that provides them.

In addition to the sites, there may also be true applications, both in the form of computer software (desktop PC) and mobile devices (smartphones and tablets) in the form of an app. In this case, the skills required for their development are even greater, and once again there will be a need for promotion to make them known and updated over time to correct any stability and security bugs or improve their functionality making them even more attractive. Of this second sector are, of course, also the games, often proposed with a freemium formula and distributed as an app or inserted into websites (e.g. in gambling or multi-user games) or on social networks. Probably those who read will have already had the opportunity to play some of these games, or to take advantage of some services like those listed above.

At this point, it will be clearer what we mean when we say that there is no passive income, a concept that we will find even later, and it is, therefore, important to underline.

2. Passive income from the sale of contents

When we talk about content, we refer not only to those that form an ebook or a book, but also to images that a photographer can sell on sites specialized in stock images, or to video and to the audio sold in the same way. In all these cases, passive income streams will derive from the repeated sale of each content, which may produce a proper revenue if it is conducted on its own or partial if sold through a distribution platform. The latter are represented, for example, by traditional bookstores or those online in the case of books and ebooks, from the already mentioned sites that sell images (photos and drawings), video or audio for professional purposes such as the development of sites or multimedia products, or again from sites that host, for example, online courses if the contents already mentioned represent, for example, a video course or an audio course.

In all these cases, the content must be produced only

once and then placed on the market through an automated sales system, and this is how the flow of passive income is created resulting from its sale. As can be understood, even for content, promotion and marketing are essential if we want to increase sales rather than simply wait for someone to notice them and buy them (something that happens), and for those contents that are subject to obsolescence (for example, courses on technical subjects) it is also necessary to proceed with periodic updates so that they remain attractive to the public and do not become too old (and therefore no longer valid) because someone decides to buy them again.

A strategy often used by those who live from the production of content is to offer a part (or a 'fragmented' version) for free, for example through a site or a blog, and create parallel commercial versions that collect them as a book/ebook, full course, and so on. In this way, it becomes possible to create a 'showcase' able to support the commercially distributed 'works,' and thus increase sales.

3. Passive income from affiliate marketing

If you do not want to sell your services, products or

content, you can always do it with those of others by earning a percentage of those sales and thus creating another form of passive income. In this case, however, the sale takes place outside of your site, directly on that of the seller. In America, the opportunities for affiliation are many and offer ample earning space.

Passive affiliate streams of income can also derive from sources other than a website, for example from content published on social networks, but in this case they have a shorter duration in time as they go into the background as time passes and it becomes less likely that the public will notice them and click on the respective links (unless you periodically invest in paid visibility, as you do for example on Facebook, highlighting the payment of a post, but in this case we will fall into passive generated by a cash investment, however minimal, so it is not appropriate to include it in this chapter. Do not worry; we will talk about passive streams of income that require a monetary investment in the next chapter.

4. Passive returns from other monetization of contents

The latter category may include, for example, services

such as the sale, or rather the rental of advertising space on a site or app that enjoys a certain popularity/visibility. The advertising spaces can be represented by text in a directory, by banners or entire pages, as happens for example in the sites/portals that are positioned in the tourism sector and rent a space to managers of hotels, restaurants, and similar activities inside of strategic areas of the site. What has just been said at the end of the previous paragraph is more valid than ever in such a field, given that advertisers will be more likely to pay their periodic share the more they are certain of gaining visibility through the site.

The same applies to the app, once they have achieved the necessary popularity, but the latter typically require investments in marketing and advertising to gain visibility among the public.

This type of passive income should not be confused with income generated through systems such as those used by portals like TripAdvisor, obviously, as in this case, it is an automated service and therefore falls into the first type of online passive income described in this chapter.

Chapter 5

Investing in Real Estate

The activity of a real estate investor is often misunderstood. Most people, when hearing the term "real estate investor" think "ok, who does this job earns a lot of money, it is fun, it is easy to do, and it is all sunshine and rainbows," but the reality is not like that. At all. This information that is disseminated all around the internet is not correct. The activity carried out by a real estate investor is a methodical activity, it is an activity that takes a long time to master. The investors have to do a lot of visits to real estates; he has to make a lot of proposals knowing that most of these offers will be rejected, as you can imagine.

It is important to operate with a large number of real estate visits and proposals to obtain results. In other words, the idea that the real estate investor walks and makes money is absolutely false; it is a very difficult job.

What I would like to tell you is that this is an extraordinary profession, where you can obtain a very important personal and economic satisfaction, but it is necessary to work hard. It is necessary to have a lot of time, and it is necessary to know from the beginning that it will not be easy. If you could automatically earn, everybody would do it, which is not real, we know it very well. To do something and get a result you need to commit, so if you are interested in the world of real estate investments, you must know that it is a difficult job like all other investments. It is a job where you'll have to spend time, where most of the answers you receive will be no, you will not have to give up, you'll have to continue and if you manage to be consistent and do things the right way you will be able to clearly get results not only at the economic level but also at the level of personal satisfaction.

Before getting started with the 15 Golden lessons of real estate investing, it is important to make a quick note about mindset.

Your dream house is not an investment, did you know that?

The property owned, or the house of our dreams - or villa depends on the possibilities of each of us, has always been considered a sacred "asset" in America. A goal to be achieved as soon as possible at the cost of any sacrifice. And indeed, we are the people with the highest percentage of homeowners. About 80% of Americans own a home. It does not matter if we take out mortgages for thirty years (sometimes even longer) with monstrous installments that most often absorb around 50% of the income of an average family. The important thing is to "own" our home. Good, this is what smart people do, right? False. Almost nobody that is rich lives in a place he owns. As Grant Cardone says "rent where you live and own what you can rent."

The question I want to ask you now is this: do you think buying a house is equivalent to buying an asset or a liability? The answer is clear and not debatable. Among the mortgage payment, various charges, government, and municipal taxes, when buying a house, you buy a liability.

But we better explain the concept of liability. By liability, we mean everything that generates cash outflow from our family income statement. In contrast, by asset, we mean everything that generates positive cash flow. Example, I buy an obligation that usually brings a coupon, this coupon represents an income, and therefore the obligation is an asset.

The sad truth of the American real estate market

But how strange: we make so many sacrifices to buy a house, yet we buy a liability? Yes, dear readers, in America, unfortunately, the investment property is almost completely unknown. In fact, there is no real estate market in the true sense of the word. And for the real estate market I mean the sale of an asset, in this case, the house, in order to realize a capital gain and therefore an investment income. Trades usually in America in the vast majority of cases are made because a couple decides to get married and then buy a house, or move after the coming of children, etc. In summary, following a family necessity and not for investing, as usually happens for financial or business investments

The ventures of real estate investing

But at this point, the question to be asked is this: is it possible to transform the purchase of a house from a liability into an asset and consequently obtain a monthly income or make a capital gain? Well, dear readers, the answer is fortunately yes! Not only is it possible, but it is desirable that each of us in the investment process of their assets dedicate part of the capital to real estate investments.

Real estate investing has some notable advantages, for example, it is possible to receive monthly income (rents) and at the same time realize capital gains at the time of sale. Not only. Precisely because of the characteristics of the market in consideration, such as the American one, the investment in real estate, is a more than secure investment, as the "home" good in America will hardly lose value.

The recent crisis has confirmed this theory. Practically in the whole world, the real estate market has undergone very heavy devaluations even in the order of 50-60%, not only in America but also in Spain, England, etc. In America, in fact, there was only a stagnation of prices and a lengthening of the time of purchase. But in fact, the market has not fallen below 5% (obviously should be made distinctions according to regions, city type of properties, central or peripheral, etc...)

Now it is time to take a look at 15 lessons to invest in real estate.

● **Invest in houses that you will rent**

We hypothesize to buy a house of $ 200,000 with a minimum investment of $ 40,000 (but some banks also finance 100% of the amount) and that with the rent we cover only the mortgage payment. Well, after ten years assuming an average revaluation of 4%, our house has been revalued for a value of $ 296,000, which means that $ 40,000 has become 96,000 in 10 years. In practice, an annual profit of 14%. Not bad, I would say if compared to the yields of bonds and some liquidity/money funds that fill the wallets of Italian savers.

In reality, the above calculations are not complete as

they do not consider the purchase and sale charges (taxes, notary, etc...) and the additional capital gain. In fact, paying the instalment of the silent, the tenant also pays us a portion of the capital loaned by the bank; which means that when we sell, in addition to the revaluation of $ 96,000, we will have to add the missing principal amount to be returned to the bank net of transaction costs.

● From liability to asset

We hypothesize that we managed to buy a good deal and that therefore the property, net of the mortgage and the charges, generates a small monthly income deriving from the rent. Suddenly what was a liability becomes a monthly income, even if only a few hundred dollars, it is an addition to your income.

● Buy only amazing deals, especially at the beginning

In order for the rent to exceed the installment of the silent, it is necessary to buy well. Buying a good deal means essentially at a good price. Opportunities are there; they simply have to be found. Some small suggestions:

- Avoid the agencies;

- Find private vendors;

- Walk around the neighborhoods that interest you looking for property for sale;

- Talk to the doorkeepers;

- Attend the Auctions in court. For the moment, it is enough to know that the system has become absolutely transparent and secure. So, you have to find the right opportunity. You can buy houses even with 30/40% discount on the real value;

- Read the announcements and identify the "needy" people to sell;

- Buy in central and/or valuable areas. It is the only guarantee for not having a bad surprise.

- **Apply leverage on your money**

Fundamental. We have seen that buying a house with an initial investment could even generate a monthly income. Well, let's imagine to replicate the investment with the same characteristics at least three times, and we hypothesize to be able to get 300 / month from each of our rents (net of charges and taxes). In fact, with $ 900 / month of capital gain we can safely pay a good installment of a mortgage for the purchase of another house, and here comes the nice, paid entirely with the revenue from the rents. I leave you the imagination of how many times it is possible to replicate the above investment scheme and calculate the benefits. It is just amazing.

- **Only take mortgages with fix interest rates**

When you engage in real estate investing, you are already taking a "business" risk; you do not need to take other risks, such as interest rate related risk. Let me explain better when buying an investment property, I need to know exactly how much is the monthly exit (installment + charges) in order to correctly calculate the expected cash flow. Only careful planning of income and expenses can lead to a correct real estate investment. The accuracy of the calculations can make the difference between a successful and a non-profitable investment.

- **Understand the peculiarity of the real estate market**

The "brick," as the real estate market was called fifty

years ago, and as still calls it some nostalgic of the Sixties, is a market like any other. Remember: in finance, there is never a 100% safe investment! Each market has its peculiarities, has its ups and downs and even the real estate market is a market that does not escape these logics. Investing in bricks can be useful and can offer interesting perspectives, but it is good that you first inform yourself before taking this step.

Do not limit yourself to looking at stock prices, but if you plan to buy an apartment or a box or another property, take a trip around the area. Consult the prices displayed outside the various real estate agencies in the district and compare them: often, even within the same city, prices change significantly from district to district. This happens because the costs of a real estate property are closely linked to the area in which it is built: if it is in the suburbs it will cost less than an identical property but located in the city center.

Furthermore, prices are also dependent on so-called connected services. For example: a three-room apartment has a certain cost if it is located in a condominium where there is a garden with its green care service by a specialized company, or there is a concierge service; an apartment with the exact same size but placed in a condominium without a green care service or porter will have a lower price.

Learn what is best to buy and what to stay away from

The very first choice that can be made, in terms of buying real estate as an investment, is certainly buying a small apartment - a studio or a two-room apartment, in short - that is located in a central area, well served by public transport, and that has at least one connected parking space, if not a garage, and this would be the best solution. Why this advice?

A small apartment is much easier to rent than a large one. Leasing an apartment to a family is very risky: you can go to cases of insolvency, and if there are children in the family, submit an injunction to eviction not only can be very complicated but you may not even be able to free your apartment. And so, you would find yourself in the unpleasant situation of not being able to dispose of your assets and having to deal with insolvent tenants: they are two big problems, as you can imagine.

Instead, a studio or a two-room apartment can be

rented to a professional who has moved to the city for work reasons. A person who does not have a dependent family but has a solid salary behind him is a guarantee of solvency and also, if the apartment you need or decide that it is time to resell it, you would have no difficulty in freeing it within the established time frame. If the studio can also combine a parking space - even if, we repeat, the box is the best solution - the added value of your property grows, especially if it is located in an area where parking can be a problem: with a value-added more, you can ask for a slightly larger rent. But you are still careful not to propose a fee outside of the logic of the market! You would risk never having a tenant, and then you would not even have an income.

Finally, a consideration on the location of the studio: central area and served by public transport. The central area because - usually - the city centres are lively areas, with rich proposals for both day and nightlife; but it is essential that there is also an excellent public transport service in the proximity of your apartment so that future tenants, if they do not want to use the car for movements, would still have the opportunity to go anywhere.

3. **Studying other real estate opportunities**

The box is a very interesting alternative to a standard one room apartment. First of all, the costs of a box are much, much smaller than those of an apartment, and this is an advantage. Even if there were extraordinary condo fees in the complex where your garage is located, the rates for you would be very low, because proportionate to the small number of thousandths of which you are the owner. Moreover, when buying a box, you should not worry about expenses related to the makeover and upholding of the domestic systems nor should you worry about restructuring or upgrading costs of sorts.

And then, if you make the smart choice to buy a box in an area where there is a lot of parking, you may have a very high probability of renting it. And not only that: you could find tenants very quickly; the replacement would be guaranteed in a very short time. Last but not least, the purchase of a box provides for a lower initial expenditure than that of an apartment: this means that, by renting it, you would be more quickly covered in expenses incurred.

4. **Always look for the right deal and not the right property**

Many investors in real estate investments are influenced by their feelings. A property is not money. You can see it, touch it, you can like it or not, and all this affects our taste, our feelings precisely, going to compromise what our brain would say instead. To be able to be objective we must detach from the building, and we must focus on our real goal, the deal. We must estrange from the property itself and look at all the economic aspects (cost, estimated costs of maintenance, condominium costs, classification value and cadastral income that affect taxes, commercial compatibility of the property and the area in which it is located in its market), it is clear that a beautiful property in a beautiful area can affect our senses more than a sad apartment in a suburban area, but often in suburban residential areas can be obtained at low costs, excellent profits, and continuity. Sometimes we strive to be objective but when we fall in love with something that objectivity fails without us even realizing it, it is at this moment that the role of our real estate consultant (that brings us back to the reality of the business, making us awaken from that 'falling in love) can be decisive in preventing us from making a mistake that could cost us a bad deal.

5. **The income from a building must be seen in the continuity of the long-term**

Sometimes when assessing the profitability of a property, you look only at the maximum peak that the property can make without taking into account the time needed to make that property profitable.

Let's take a classic example, small property in a highly residential area of high value, clearly it is a building that can produce a high return and many dwell only on this without taking into account the fact that it is a property that can be used for short periods giving long breaks in which the income becomes a cost (tax, condominium), it is necessary time or costs (of real estate agencies) to get that income and can also be incurred more often than the maintenance costs in addition to risking more easily the problematic situations or arrears that, although kept under control with the right tools, lead at least to an increase of time to devote to the problem (if not incurred expenses or lost revenue).

6. The real estate deal is made at the time of purchase and not of sale

Those who can buy with a substantial discount will never make mistakes. It may not be the most easily marketable building on the market, but when you have a substantial margin to sell it, everything becomes much simpler, safer and more profitable.

On the contrary, those who buy without getting a good discounted deal, that is at market price, counting on the fact that the market will rise, can easily find themselves in an uncomfortable position, given that even in a situation like the current one where prices are low and is actually the time to buy to do business, certainties about a further downturn or a safe short-term recovery do not exist, while those who buy below cost have the certainty of being able to resell at least the market price that would allow them to make a profit (which if then the market goes up can become an exceptional profit).

But at this point, the question is *how do you buy at a discounted price?* The answer is simple, you must look (and the market is always full of them, but especially in times of crisis like these) for a motivated seller, or someone who wants to sell, who no longer wants to keep that property, for any given reason. It is useless to waste time with someone who has time or money and wants to make the maximum profit. On the other hand, you should always look for (and how many there are around today!) someone who does not have time and maybe even money. It will certainly be a motivated seller and ready to buy with a substantial discount your real estate deal.

7. **Learn how to set up and conduct a negotiation**

There are various factors ranging from experience and skills in the industry: from personal attitude (it's a bit like the good poker player who must have innate qualities to be able to bluff and bring his opponent straight to the goal that has been set, and other qualities that will instead refine with time and experience) to coldness and impartiality with respect to the affair.

It is clear that a good consultant will have all these characteristics being an expert who knows the techniques to be used in a negotiation, for example, a simple but always effective rule to follow is to never say a price first. It is statistically proven that the first to make a price by discovering, even if partially, their cards will eventually have a good chance of making the worst deal. The same building may be worth very different prices that depend fundamentally on the specific negotiating position of the parties and the respective ability to know how to negotiate. But a good consultant will also have the enormous advantage over the counterpart (and the investor represented) to be a third party, cold compared to the property and the deal, ready to lose the property and even the deal (if the deal no longer detecting oneself) without those guilt and loss senses that strike those who are about to reach the coveted object and suddenly see it slip out of hand (a certain element that often leads one of the parties when in negotiation personally to give up at a point or memento that will cost him inexorably a large part or all of his own profit), without considering that the third party consultant will have more chances to influence the counterpart towards his objective of the part that will always be seen as an antagonist.

8. **Being able to buy without or with very little money and zero risk**

The most substantial real estate profit is always

without costs with huge advantages compared to investing with money. So always buy with as little money as possible, or even better, without your own money.

Do you have a bank fund? Of course, it is possible, but unless you are in relationships or positions such that the lenders offer you easy money at very low costs or conditions, which happens in very few cases for very few categories of investors, the Banks, for costs and conditions imposed, are the worst way to get the necessary money for your investment.

The solution is to charge your real estate investment to three different parties, either alternatively or cumulatively. The first is a subject interested in living in the building, a formula that is increasingly successful is the rent with redemption, a form of atypical contract (which with the use is, however, being typed) that mixes lease and sale. Imagine finding a seller who, in order to get rid of the property, is willing to rent it with a redemption (today as there are always more rumors given the spread of the phenomenon and the difficulty of selling otherwise). We could propose a similar formula but more advantageous (fiscally) to this seller, we imagine proposing a preliminary contract with a payment in installments (at three years if we want more transcription if we are not interested in transcribing), the seller accepts (becoming, in fact, our second investor) attracted by the possibility of getting rid of the property (or at least to forfeit the deposit after three years) and above all to get rid of expenses and of the real estate taxation that belongs to the owner, we investors do not spend a dollar: we limit ourselves to finding a tenant (the one who pays our real estate investment) that occupies the property. You deliver the money to be transferred to the owner in installment as a deposit (as well as advance on the price), and at the end of the three years (or longer period agreed), we will have (without having spent a single dollar) the possibility of buying a property whose price has already been partially paid with that deposit actually paid by the tenant, now being able to evaluate if in the past years the market is climbed, and the property has been appreciated or not we will have 3 possibilities abstractly verifiable:

- The market has grown, and the property has appreciated. We hypothesize a property for which at the time was agreed on the price of

500 thousand dollars of which 50 thousand already paid in the form of installment, we imagine that the property is worth 600 thousand today we can pay it 450 thousand (or we can offer the purchase, if we do not have money available to a financing partner, third party that could finance our real estate investment, which paid it in full or in part based on its real value of 600 thousand allows us to conclude an excellent profit, with certainty and without risk our money if not at the end and minimally).

- The market has remained stable, so in our example, the property is still worth 500 thousand, but we will pay 450 thousand, being a part already paid by our tenant. In this case, however, we will have made a good profit, although not as exceptional as in the previous case.

- The market has dropped a lot. It is the worst case scenario in which if we had invested our money we would have made a substantial loss or we should keep the property locked for years waiting for better times, but with our strategy, we can decide not to buy the property, without losing anything, the deposit will, in fact, be paid by our tenant, and we were able to exit at no cost from the worst situation that could happen, virtually eliminating risks and losses.

The exemplified use of the preliminary contract and the deposit is only one of the many examples that explain how the knowledge of contracts and real estate tax that every real good real estate consultant should know can bring a lot of value to the new investor.

9. Learn how to save money on the investment

At a time like this when the tax oppression has reached, in all sectors (and especially in the real estate industry), a very high level, the result of any investment can never reach (except in exceptional cases) the return that can be guaranteed by significant tax savings. So, if the real estate profit that I can go to realize can also be halved by the weight of the tax, it is clear that I, if I find the way to avoid that tax oppression (or at least reduce it enormously), I can have a higher profit. So, the golden rule is to find the way to adopt those contractual-tax measures (and there are really dozens of atypical contracts usable in this regard) that can, through the tax lever, double your real estate profit

10. **You do not have to be an expert to get returns on your real estate investments**

Very true. In fact, Warren Buffett is not an expert in real estate, let alone is an expert in farms or shopping centers. So how did you invest and achieve these results even if you are not an expert? The reason is simple. Warren Buffett knows the rules of investments and applies them in all fields: on the stock exchange, in real estate, in the business. Warren Buffett knows how to recognize an investment opportunity, take action and close a big deal.

That is why even a person who is not an expert in real estate can invest and earn a lot: because you do not need to be an expert, but you must know the rules of the game, or the basis of investment, and these can be learned by anyone, even from those who do not believe it is possible to learn them. The next step is then to put these notions and strategies into practice. The result? You will get results, just like Warren Buffett has been doing for decades. Not a bad perspective, right?

In this part of the book, we talk about houses, rents and real estate, with the aim of finally debunking the myth linked to real estate investment.

Also, because, unlike what you hear around, there are still some situations where you can invest in real estate and bring home a good performance, but this is only true in some special cases and above all under certain conditions.

What I can guarantee is that it is not a simple and trivial activity, as those who do not have experience, skills or simply want to take advantage of it want to make you believe.

On this topic I think that one of the most repeated phrases in absolute is:

"Brick is an excellent investment. It is safe and never betrays. The value of the property always grows over time ".

But as you probably noticed, you are not exactly like that, as the price of houses has fallen considerably over the last few years.

We must, therefore, try to overcome popular beliefs and give an adequate answer to the question of the questions, namely:

Is it still worthwhile investing in properties today?

And to solve this doubt we can not rely on "hearsay" or "bar opinions," but we must rather rely on a serious and documented analysis of how things are.
Every time I talk to someone with money, in 99% of cases we end up talking about real estate.

"That one is so rich that he owns the whole city."

"That guy collects an avalanche of money every month through his properties."

These and other similar discourses are generally used to indicate the wealth of people who, in the popular imagination, have built a fortune thanks to the brick.

To this is added the literature Made in USA that, if you are minimally interested in business, economic growth or finance, you inevitably have to read also, like the various Kiyosaki & co., Just to name a few, who have built their notoriety about the leitmotif "buy real estate and enrich yourself".

Investing in real estate: a safe investment after all?

If you talk about buying a big car, many may wonder if you actually can afford to keep it.

If you go on vacation with a certain frequency, someone mumbles that you are a spendthrift.

Even worse if you rely on an independent financial advisor or if you open a trading account to make investments.

They immediately label you as crazy!

However, if you declare that you have bought a $ 250,000 apartment to go and live or if you have purchased a property that is falling apart in the suburbs of the world, compliments are in abundance, and nobody doubts the goodness of your choice.

This is because we are used to thinking that real estate investment is as safe as a government bond.

"The grandfather has paid the house 2 million; today is worth 200,000 dollars" (inflation, for heaven's sake, let's not go down that route please!).

Here is just one of the many data that you can check yourself on the progress of our "safe investment" from 2007 to 2016.
The value of real estate has plummeted over a single decade (-28% in the best case).

Probably we are touching the fund and then go back, but the fact remains that those who bought in the pre-economic crisis, i.e., in the collective euphoria of the race to the brick, today saw the value of its investment strongly depreciated.
Who has needed to get rid of their purchase has sold off or has remained with the weight on the rump for years, given the absence of a flourishing market ready to win the apartment.

The old reasoning on the security of real estate purchase collides with the harsh reality of the world that has changed significantly.
If your relatives bought in the post-war period, when

there was a company to be rebuilt from scratch, and so many cities practically did not exist, it is quite obvious to say that there has been a re-evaluation.

First, there were the stones, 30 years later there were cities. Until the 70s the population was young and procreated at great rates. From the 1990s onwards, population growth, in line with other Western countries, has been miserably arrested, only to reverse the trend.

We are always the same, we are older, and there are no more avalanches of people and families willing to move, change cities and enrich the demand for apartments.

According to The American Institute of Public Opinions, today 80% of Americans live in a house owned, that is, the same Italians who are old and therefore do not move, do not have children and, all in all, can always stay in the first apartment in which they entered. In a nutshell, anyone who could buy a house has already done it.

All others either are not owners by choice or simply can not afford it and must live in rent.

The legislation on leases, among other things, is very unbalanced in favor of the tenants and getting a bad guy, in a historical era of changes and difficulties in employment, has become more frequent than anything else.

All this leads to a dutiful reflection.

If almost everyone has a home in which to live, if we are on average less young and less likely to travel, if we have now almost all poured near large urban centers leaving the suburbs, how can we think of a growth propulsive real estate market in the coming decades?

Well, now that I slapped you and I made you understand why the adage "the brick is a safe investment" is a commonplace of the past, we can try to understand when it becomes convenient by doing two calculations together.

Also because the fact that it is not so sure does not

mean that there are no opportunities to be seized.

Investing in real estate: opportunities are there and will always be there

I wanted to warn you before entering the heart of the discussion.

After a brainstorming of negative things, we come to the opportunities that the sector offers at this time.

First point: prices are at historic lows.

The collapse of prices can be a pain for those who sell, but an opportunity for those who buy.

Every market has its precise movements and lives of ups and downs, and even the real estate is not immune to all this. Specifically, in the real estate market, there are many people who, unfortunately, must sell because they have immediate liquidity needs.

If we add this aspect to the already huge amount of property in circulation, this means that, as there is so much offer, you can buy at relatively low prices compared to the past.

From this point of view, many innovations are also spreading in America.

Short term rentals are on the rise thanks to the explosion of portals such as Airbnb and Home Away. Thanks to the diffusion of cheap means of transport, people who go on holiday have increased considerably and do not disdain to stay in apartments rather than in hotels. Tourism in our country, overall, is in excellent health. According to the MIBACT statistical office, last year we exceeded the threshold of 50 million visitors and recorded an increase of about 5 million visitors compared to 2016.

Although our universities are not among the best in the world, they attract students from all over the country. From the outskirts to the cities, from the South to the North, every year many off-site students move to get their degree. In short, the question is there, but obviously, it is necessary to act selectively going to grasp the potential that only some areas, and not all without distinction, can offer.

Let me explain to you better what I mean by this statement.

The main tourist resorts will never go into crisis, and the short rental market is quite benevolent with the owner because he does not have the familiar difficulties.

Large cities attract tourists, students, and workers who generally offer greater guarantees and with whom it is possible to sign contracts with shorter duration and, therefore, less exposed to the risks of residential rent.

Above all the centers of big cities are often the object of a specular development with respect to the suburbs, which become impoverished and depopulated.

People, especially wealthy people, prefer services to the isolation of remote areas.

In short, investing in real estate is still possible, if you know how to do it!

Investing in real estate: let's do the maths!
Enough words, let's move on to the numbers.

I want to share with you the analysis I did in the summer of 2017, thinking about New York.

My hypothesis is based on the purchase of a property located in a strategic area because it is very close to the main university.

The idea of exploiting the investment is based on renting out-of-town students who come to the city to study.
The area I am talking about is well served by public transport and is quite lively from a commercial point of view. The district is largely inhabited by families, the elderly, workers or students. The rental market can be said to be good enough for the reason that ruled my choice.

Speaking of numbers, the price per square meter varies from $ 1,000 for properties to be completely renovated, up to $ 1,800 for apartments in good condition and ready to be inhabited. Wanting for a moment to estimate to be good negotiators, we can concretely think of bringing home a two-bedroom apartment to renovate with $ 50,000. Obviously, we are also building experts, and we select an apartment that, in the fundamentals, is in good condition. You do not have to redo the systems, you just have to repaint, you have to replace the sanitary, and you have to change the floor in one of the rooms.

In light of my experience, I can tell you that the cost of the work is around $ 10,000.

We set a maximum ceiling of $ 8,000 and let us venture to IKEA.

To finance the operation, I stick to what all the books say about financial growth: select the mortgage which, among other things, is given you at a very low rate.
After all, we are taught by American gurus and local popularizers, in which other sectors we lend the money to 2-3%?

If you are an entrepreneur like me and sometimes you have come to the bank to ask for money, you know exactly what I am talking about.
The bank will finance 80% of the work because today 100% mortgages are rare if you do not have a particular history.
However, since we are good and credible, the bank also finances the work partly, so on $ 60,000 of

spending we receive a loan of $ 48,000.

I tried to pull down estimates for a twenty-year mortgage, and the lowest provides a monthly payment of $ 234.95 in 20 years, with costs of investigation of $ 850 and appraisal for $ 320

To this, you must add other additional expenses such as:

- Compulsory house cover: the annual cost that I estimate is about $ 240 which makes $ 4,800 for 20 years;
- Life insurance: bad luck aside, one cannot be exposed to the risk of leaving debts to the heirs. I estimated a cost based on my age (27 years) and a capital of $ 50,000 I assure you with about $ 80 per year ($ 1,600 total in 20 years) if you have a few years more than me you could pay a little 'more, put it in a quote;
- Disability coverage: make all the perils of the world here too, for me, safety comes first. I never went around with the scooter because I was afraid of falling, imagine if I buy a house with the risk of not having the money to make

up for the diseases. Here, too, I estimated myself and took out an annual cost of about $ 150, then $ 3,000 total over 20 years of mortgage.

Calm, it's not over yet. At these expenses you must add:

- Real Estate Agency commission: on a purchase of this type you must estimate at least $ 3,500;
- Notarial deed: the costs are at your expense, you must pay both the deed of sale and the deed of loan, for the joy of the notary of the rogant. At least $ 4,000 are needed;
- Registry tax: in short, if you buy as a first home pay less but, as an investment, we must rule out this hypothesis because you will not go there to live. The purchase, therefore, you do it as a second home and, therefore, pay the beauty of 9% that corresponds to $ 4,500.

To sum up, the total cost of the operation is:

- $ 56.388 (total to be returned to the bank) +

- $ 8,000 (furniture) +
- $ 850 (preliminary investigation) +
- $ 320 (appraisal) +
- $ 4,800 (home coverage) +
- $ 1,600 (life insurance) +
- $ 3,000 (disability coverage) +
- $ 3,500 (agency) +
- $ 4,000 (notary) +
- $ 4,500 (registration tax) = $ 86,958

Without going into the merits of what you have to pay right away and what instead extensions over time, the operation costs you $ 4,337.90 per year (total divided into 20 years of mortgage), i.e. $ 362.33 per month.

Now we calculate the expenses of your competence, i.e. those that you must take out of your pocket and immediately:

- $ 12,000 (advance 20%) +
- $ 8,000 (furniture) +
- $ 1,170 (appraisal and investigation) +
- $ 3,500 (real estate agency) +
- $ 4,000 (notary) +
- $ 4,500 (taxes) =

- $ 33,170 is the capital you need to start the operation.

Now that we have done the calculations on the expense, we come to the lease of the property.

We want to make it to students, so in the two-room apartment, we create two beds that we make at $ 350 each, for a monthly income of $ 700, which makes $ 8,400 gross annual income.

Let us simplify and pretend to rent without an agency, the costs charged to us are the dry coupon, which immediately declines 21% of the rent (which falls to 6.636 $) and condo and maintenance fees that, again to simplify, I esteem in $ 1,500 per year.

There is $ 5,136 net.

Considering the weighted annual cost, the net profit is $ 788.10 ($ 5.136 - $ 4.347.90).

You are awake, however, and you have taken out the loan for the purchase, letting you lend the money from the bank.

In this case, the calculation on the return of the real

estate investment must, therefore, be based on the actual return generated by your capital, net of the installment to be paid to the bank.

Technically speaking we are talking about ROE, that is the acronym of Return on Equity, where "equity" is the Capital, that is the one that you pour from your pocket.

The calculation of the ROE is done with this formula:

(Net Annual Income / Own Capital) * 100

We, therefore, calculate the Net Annual Income.

$ 5.136 - $ 2.819.40 (mortgage payment) - $ 470 (annual cost of insurance) = $ 1.846 annuity.

As for Capital Just, you have spent $ 33,170 to start everything.

So, if we put the data in the formula we find: (1.846 / 33.170) * 100 = 5.56%

Congratulations, you have earned 5.56% on your investment property, and you did better than American government bonds that do not reach 2%.

Am I wrong or have you read something similar even in the newspapers?

Well, they're all false information, and I'll explain why.

Investing in real estate: it is a profession, not an investment

As I begin to write this last paragraph, I look at the clock: 2 hours have passed since I started to reckon.

It took 2 hours just to plan; I dare not imagine even the time it would take if I wanted to do it in practice.

If you are an entrepreneur or a professional you are used to reasoning according to the time value of your time, so just try to calculate the number of hours needed to plan, organize and manage all this, which can generate (when and if all goes well) an income of around $ 2,000 per year.

And I have not even tried to imagine the value of income if, instead of going to the bank, I had bought with my own money.

At this point, you could tell me that my calculations are wrong because you would be able to cut many expenses and maximize profits.

Good boy. Compliments. Welcome to the entrepreneurs' world.

The difference between an investment and a business activity lies in the time it takes. I invest my money to make it work for me; I can even help a professional who drives me but I do not use 50, 100 or 200 hours per year to follow my investments.

The reality is much more complex and often full of contingencies and (small or large) errors of assessment. With all the variables we have seen, the chances of loss are not so remote. Moreover, since this is a business activity in all respects, the risks are high, as they must justify the potential high returns.

So, I'm the one who's going to turn the question to you now.

Are you still sure that investing in brick is a safe and sound deal?

As you can see, once the fog blanket and the ham on the eyes have been removed, it is immediately clear that this is an operation that has its degree of complexity, as well as a certain amount of (right) risks.

As such, you must treat it in the same way you approach your work.

You have to spend time, a lot of time, to do your analysis, the checks, the calculations of the case and the resolution of the small problems that will inevitably arise.

Furthermore, you must also bear the burden of "entrepreneurial" risks linked to the particular dynamics of this type of market.

Having said that, we have seen that there are still opportunities, even if they have to be selected with greater attention and precision than in the past.

Chapter 6

Why Insurance Must Play A Role

To have life insurance, you must be healthy (and what you pay each year varies from many factors. You must never omit anything about your state of health to the insurance company as it may not pay coverage to the beneficiaries in case the unexpected happens to the insured. Also, insurance companies often recommend splitting insurance into two that should last 20 years (your child is five years old, and you want to cover it from the risk of loss of income until the hypothetical end of the university study path). This is explained to you as an advantage in financial terms. The advantage is there because you save some money. But you must dwell on the final purpose of TCM. In your opinion, is it to gain or protect those dear to you from your lack? Exactly the second answer is the right one! So, returning to the example what would happen if your health conditions worsen when your first 10-year insurance expires and the insurance company does not make you a new TCM for the next ten years? Nothing at all! You have to cross your fingers and hope to have accumulated enough to make your child survive better, hoping to be able to enroll him at the university! So, forget if you want to make money with TCM. By their nature they only serve to protect your loved ones and to get rid of the most feared question: and if I will not be there next year, who will take care of my family?

So, the TCM, like many other types of insurance (there are 24 insurance branches provided for by the Insurance Code), are used to avoid unpleasant surprises in the future. These risks, of course, are unpredictable and I do not expect them to happen to anyone, and we should not try to predict them when they happen. We need only to build protection through insurance policies. To confirm this, I quote the quote from world-renowned investor Warren Buffet: "it is not necessary to predict the rain, but it is important to know how to build the Ark."

Chapter 7

Destroy Debt Forever

The best way to destroy debt forever is not to start paying it immediately but to create a business that gives you cash flow that you can use to pay off the debt. Here are some creative ways to do it.

Flipping online businesses

Flippa is the number one portal for selling and buying websites: it boasts a huge audience and offers excellent tools to increase the visibility of your online auction. If you are going to commit a bit of capital, a little time and a lot of "rags," the buying and selling of sites on Flippa could bring you great profits and build, over time, a nice income stream.

The platform has sold sites for 140 million dollars

since the launch in 2009. If you want to contribute to increasing this amount, you should read the following pages.

Find a niche

Before investing a single euro or dollar, you must be clear about what your site will look like and what it will talk about. In this phase, it is good to find a niche with potential and start from that. Alternatively, if you think you know about a certain topic that can be considered a niche, then design the blog in that direction.

Focusing on a specific "small" sector is already a first step in cutting out large numbers of competitors. Obviously, the niche must have at least a little bit of a client base, you do not want to work for nothing, right?

Building Vs. Buying

Well, you found your industry, now it's about securing a site, and then the doubt that arises is build it or buy it? Let's see what are the pros and cons of both cases.

1. Build your site

Unless you're a web developer, creating a site from scratch can cost you a few hundred dollars - unless you buy one already existing, anyway. You can also follow an ad hoc course, but the quickest way is definitely to hire a programmer who does the "dirty work" and build your blog on a solid foundation.

It would be good to create it on WordPress. Those who buy websites, generally, know this platform and therefore tend to buy preferably WordPress sites. Once the site is set up, you need content that is focused on keywords and full of affiliate links.

The ways to follow are essentially two: either you create all the content or pay someone to do it for you. Sites like Fiverr put you in touch with copywriters, writers, graphic designers and much more (the texts cost an average of $5 for 500 words).

When you have accumulated a lot of material, avoid publishing it all in one step and dilute it over time, following the classical one/two articles per day patter.

2. Buy your site

Very often buying a site already started will cost you more than creating it from scratch, but at the same time, you will enjoy some significant benefits. First of all, a consolidated public (more or less numerous), and according to the site will already be indexed on search engines.

The key point is to buy it for less than it actually is worth. You must be careful of at least three factors when approaching a seller of underserved sites:

- the owner does not update it very often;
- the site does not make much money;
- the owner seems disinterested in his business

If you find something with these features, consider making an offer. But if finding the "perfect site" that meets these requirements becomes too exhausting or steals too much time, you can rely on a site broker. Many of these are commissioned and have access to huge databases of sites. Just tell them the key points, and they will find the site that's right for you.

Once you have purchased the site, use all the means you have to grow it, increase traffic and earn money.

Sell sites on Flippa

When your site has achieved good traffic, engagement and financial potential it is time to put it on auction on Flippa. Here are some suggestions for creating a successful auction.

1. Prepare a detailed description

As also reported by Flippa in a blog post, the auctions that are less successful are those with little information in the descriptions. Few data available reflect the shortage of the seller and the site itself. Possible buyers might think that if you did not want to write a description, how distract can you have managed your site?

Try to write an understandable text, with a professional tone, able to generate interest and inspire security.

2. Enter the statistics

It may seem obvious, but the first thing that a possible

buyer will read will be the statistics of your site. So, make sure that they are as up-to-date as possible, especially with regard to page views and gross revenue.

3. Do not be anonymous

Try to imagine to place hundreds of dollars of an offer to a seller without a name, without a face or a social account, would you rather not know who you are dealing with? Those who buy feel much safer to negotiate with a real person, especially when the price of the site begins to be important. Your name and your face tell the buyer that you have nothing to hide and you are not a scam artist. The first thing you need to earn is your client's trust; the second is his money.

4. Reach the "most active categories" on Flippa

If your auction is very popular, Flippa could put it in the "most active" category. This does not cost you anything, but it gives you a lot of visibility, putting you in front of thousands of buyers. The advice I've given you so far should help you get more offers, but if you realize they are less than you expect, try the following.

Let's say you've launched an auction and you already received an offer in the early hours, as a seller you can decide whether to accept it or wait to receive more. Once you approve the first, the others will follow automatically. If you set aside more offers without approving them and then do it at once, Flippa's algorithm acknowledges that your auction is very busy. So, you have more chances to finish among the "Most Active" ones.

5. Create a sustainable product

How much maintenance does your site require? How much will the buyer have to work to make it profitable? Offers may stop if buyers realize that the site needs more time than it actually is worth.

So, try not to worry about them and make sure your site is sustainable. Starting from the contents, let's say that they are all floored of your lot and that have allowed you to save money. But think how the customer can react knowing that he will have to look for and hire a freelancer to create new posts.

If you have been relying on external writers right from the start, just pass them on to the new owner who will then have to deal with experienced collaborators.

6. Reach all potential buyers

Do not rely on the only offers you receive, try to be active in the search for new buyers as well. If the promotion through social media is not enough, contact directly the owners of the sites that are part of your niche. Maybe they may be interested in buying your site to increase earnings, or just to permanently eliminate competition.

Buying and selling sites on Flippa is not an activity you can do in one night, but if you invest time and energy, you can get excellent profits. Remember to buy or create a site that belongs to a profitable niche and make it grow so that it generates money. When you place the auction on Flippa make sure you take advantage of all the promotion channels and always be transparent with your potential customers.

I have always liked this business model because it allows anyone to start their little empire with little money. 100$ are often enough to create a powerful website that will attract buyers on Flippa. After you have made your first profit, it is important to use it to fuel the business and create another website to sell.

Sooner than later, you will have enough capital to outsource the creation of the sites, and you will find yourself collecting money on autopilot. How can you do it? I highly recommend visiting Upwork.com, a powerful website that allows you to find hundreds, if not thousands, of virtual assistants that can be hired for cheap (most of them work for 2-3$ per hour) and instruct them to post your listings on Flippa. I have done this before, and I really loved the freedom that outsourcing the listing part gave me. My favorite VA and the one I collaborate with to this day is Ammar Shafiq: I highly recommend him to you.

If you do not want to go down the Upwork route, you can always try to find virtual assistants of Facebook groups or on other platforms. Just keep in mind that when you are not using a centralized and controlled platform, you are more likely to bump into scammers and people that do not take things as seriously as they should.

Dropship your way out of debt

We have come to one of my favorite online business models. Dropshipping is a retail model where the store does not hold a stock of products but only buys them after the purchase from the client has already happened.

The supplier - typically a wholesaler or a manufacturer - receives the order and takes care of the shipment to the final customer, without specifying his identity. The result is that, in the eyes of the customer, the entire transaction is managed by the store that does not actually even see the product that is sold.

To better understand how it works, let's take a concrete example.

Suppose that amazinglamps.com is an online store specializing in - guess what - lamps, which operates using dropshipping with a wholesaler in the sector. When Mr.Brown decides to buy a lamp for his daughter's wedding, does a search on Google and finds a perfect lamp for her house.

This is exactly what happens, step by step.

Step 1 - Mr.Brown places an order on amazinglamps.com

Once he chose his lamp, Mr.Brown completes the purchase by making a payment of $80 with a credit card and indicating his shipping address. The payment is deposited in the account of amazinglamps.com and Mr.Brown receives an automatic confirmation email.

Step 2 - amazinglamps.com passes the order to its supplier

Together with the confirmation email addressed to Mr.Brown, the e-commerce platform of amazinglamps.com automatically sends an email to the supplier with all the order details including the item code ordered and the shipping address.

Amazinglamps.com has already left a credit card to its supplier to use for each order. The supplier, therefore, uses this card by withdrawing an amount of $50, or the cost of the lamp according to the price list reserved for amazinglamps.com.

Step 3 - The supplier sends the lamp to Mr.Brown

The supplier sends the ordered article to Mr.Brown,

using a package with the amazinglamps.com logo. Once the order has been sent, the supplier sends a confirmation email to amazinglamps.com, including the $50 invoice and the tracking number for tracking the shipment on the shipper's website.

Step 4 - amazinglamps.com warns Mr.Brown of the shipment

Once the shipping confirmation has been received from the supplier, the manager of amazinglamps.com uses its e-commerce platform to send a confirmation email to Mr.Brown.

The email also contains the tracking number and a link to the shipper's website that Mr.Brown can use to track the position of his package in real time.

Step 5, the big step - Mr.Brown receives his lamp and happily gifts it to his daughter

After a couple of days, Mr.Brown receives the package of amazinglamps.com and shows satisfied his purchase to his wife, who finds the lamp very elegant. The following week, Mr.Brown gifts the lamp to his daughter.

Despite its fundamental role, throughout the transaction, the supplier is completely invisible to Mr.Brown. On the package, there is the logo of amazinglamps.com, and there is never any reference to those involved in packaging and shipping the package.

In fact, the wholesaler is as if it did not exist for the final customer. His sole responsibility is to store the products and send them when an order is received. Everything else - development and management of the e-commerce site, marketing activities, customer service, etc. - is the responsibility of the retailer.

This model is often referred to as the ultimate solution for those who want to start an online business. Without a doubt, it is the simplest model but in fact, has its pros and cons that I want to show you one by one.

Benefits

Minimum investment - Probably the biggest advantage of dropshipping is the possibility of launching an e-commerce store without having to invest thousands of dollars for the purchase of products. With the dropshipping model, in fact, you do not have to buy any product until the moment you have already sold it, and you have already received payment from your customer. It is, therefore, possible to start a successful dropshipping business with an investment close to zero.

Easy to get started - Carrying out an e-commerce business is much easier when you are not dealing with physical products. With dropshipping you do not have to worry about:

- Managing or pay for a warehouse;
- Packing and ship your orders;
- Keeping track of inventory;
- Managing returns;
- Managing stock reorders.

Reduced expenses - Not having to deal with the advance purchase of products in the catalogue or with the management of the warehouse, your expenses are very low. You can safely run a dropshipping business from home with your laptop, spending less than $50 a month for your Shopify store plus some useful accounting tool.

As your business grows, your expenses also increase, but they will always be very low compared to those who run a traditional e-commerce or even a physical store.

Independence from the workplace - A dropshipping business can be managed from anywhere in the world as long as there is an Internet connection. All you need to do is update your site, communicate with customers and pass orders by email to suppliers. If you think about it, this aspect is very important and can literally change your life.

You will probably never work lying in a hammock on a tropical island, but the fact that you can do it will make you feel better. If nothing else, you can choose your usual place of work, away from the chaos and traffic and this will make your routine much better.

A wide range of products - Not having to buy the products you sell in advance, means that you can add to your catalog all the products that suppliers provide you with. If a product is in stock, you can sell it on your e-commerce site at no additional cost. Despite this is a great advantage, you have to be careful not to get too caught up, putting up an online superstore that sells everything. Most people prefer niche stores rather than larger ones.

Even with dropshopping, it is essential to select a specific niche that gives your business a clear and well-defined shape.

Scalability - With a traditional business, if you receive double orders, you typically have to work twice as hard to sort them out. With dropshipping, however, most of the work is done by your suppliers allowing you to grow without weighing on your shoulders too much. Especially if your processes are automated, you will actually have an increase in work only for customer service.

On Shopify there is a very popular app that allows you to put the autopilot to your online store, taking care of sorting the orders in real time to one or more of your suppliers based on the products sold.
All these benefits make dropshipping a very attractive

model for both beginners and experienced traders. Unfortunately, they are not all sunshine and rainbows.

All this convenience and flexibility has a price to pay.

Disadvantages

Low margins - The main problem with dropshipping is the low margins per order that can usually be obtained. This is because buying a product only after selling it; you can not use the same price lists that are reserved for those who buy large volumes in advance. As a result, to remain competitive and not go off-market with the selling price, you have no choice but to keep your top-ups low.

As we have seen, the perfect product to sell online has a surcharge of 500% compared to the purchase price. With dropshipping, you can forget about a margin of this kind, and you can expect to reach 30-40% at the most.

To mitigate this problem, you can always deal with your suppliers when your sales become regular and your orders, even if diluted over time, start to have important numbers. However, this will not happen in the first few months of your business, so you'll have to consider fairly tight initial earnings.

Problems with products availability - If you manage your products, it is relatively easy to track the availability of what you are selling. If on the contrary, you supply from one or more wholesalers who distribute your products to other merchants, the availability can vary very quickly within a day.

In theory, you could solve this problem by integrating with your suppliers' warehouse software, but this is not always a viable path, also because the technological equipment of your suppliers may not be as evolved as you would like.

Complex shipping costs - If you work with more than one supplier, you may have products in the same order that will be shipped from different warehouses, multiplying shipping costs.

For example, if your customer enters an order with two products belonging to two different wholesalers, two parcels must be shipped, and shipping costs will be double. To offer a quality service, you will have to pay for these additional expenses resulting in a loss on your profit margin.

Vendor errors - Have you ever been accused of something that you did not have any fault but that fell under your responsibility?

Even the best suppliers make mistakes, and when it happens, you'll have to take on all the responsibilities and apologize to your customer. Remember that in his eyes there is only your store and as well as giving you positive feedback in the case of a good shopping experience, he will complain to you in case of problems with his order.

Chapter 8

Get Rich Slow and Steady

As Grant Cardone said, "you don't want to get rich fast, you want to get rich for sure." When you are starting out, it is easy to get caught up in *get rich quick* schemes. However, the best way is to invest in stable markets and enjoy the profits in the long run. An example? The real estate market.

We have already talked about it a bit in a dedicated chapter, but we feel that there are a few specific lessons that you need to learn if you want to get rich slow and steady, that the real estate market can teach you.

Here are a few tips that you should never forget, when thinking about building your property portfolio.

1. **Understand the peculiarity of the real estate market**

The "brick", as the real estate market was called fifty years ago, and as still calls it some nostalgic of the Sixties, is a market like any other. Remember: in finance there is never a 100% safe investment! Each market has its own peculiarities, has its ups and downs and even the real estate market is a market that does not escape these logics. Investing in bricks can be useful and can offer interesting perspectives, but it is good that you first inform yourself before taking this step.

Do not limit yourself to looking at stock prices, but if you plan to buy an apartment or a box or another property, take a trip around the area. Consult the prices displayed outside the various real estate agencies in the district and compare them: often, even within the same city, prices change significantly from district to district. This happens because the costs of a real estate property are closely linked to the area in which it is built: if it is in the suburbs it will cost less than an exactly identical property but located in the city centre.

Furthermore, prices are also dependent on so-called

connected services. For example: a three-room apartment has a certain cost if it is located in a condominium where there is a garden with its green care service by a specialized company, or there is a concierge service; an apartment with the exact same size but placed in a condominium without a green care service or porter will have a lower price.

2. **Learn what is best to buy and what to stay away from**

The very first choice that can be made, in terms of buying real estate as an investment, is certainly buying a small apartment - a studio or a two-room apartment, in short - that is located in a central area, well served by public transport and that has at least one connected parking space, if not a garage, and this would be the best solution. Why this advice?

A small apartment is much more easy to rent than a large one. Leasing an apartment to a family is very risky: you can go to cases of insolvency, and if there are children in the family, submit an injunction to eviction not only can be very complicated but you may not even be able to free your apartment. And so you would find yourself in the unpleasant situation of not being able to dispose of your personal assets and having to deal with insolvent tenants: they are two big problems, as you can imagine.

Instead, a studio or a two-room apartment can be rented to a professional who has moved to the city for work reasons. A person who does not have a dependent family but has a solid salary behind him is a guarantee of solvency and also, if the apartment you need or decide that it is time to resell it, you would have no difficulty in freeing it within the established time frame. If the studio can also combine a parking space - even if, we repeat, the box is the best solution - the added value of your property grows, especially if it is located in an area where parking can be a problem: with a value added more, you can ask for a slightly larger rent. But you are still careful not to propose a fee outside of the logic of the market! You would risk never having a tenant, and then you would not even have an income.

Finally, a consideration on the location of the studio: central area and served by public transport. The central area because - usually - the city centres are lively areas, with rich proposals for both day and night life; but it is essential that there is also an excellent public transport service in the proximity of your apartment so that future tenants, if they do not want to use the car for movements, would still have the opportunity to go anywhere.

3. **Studying other real estate opportunities**

The box is a very interesting alternative to a standard one room apartment. First of all, the costs of a box are much, much smaller than those of an apartment, and this is definitely an advantage. Even if there were extraordinary condo fees in the complex where your garage is located, the rates for you would be very low, because proportionate to the small number of thousandths of which you are the owner. Moreover, when buying a box you should not worry about expenses related to the makeover and upholding of the domestic systems nor should you worry about restructuring or upgrading costs of sorts.

And then, if you make the smart choice to buy a box in an area where there is a lot of parking, you may have a very high probability of renting it. And not only that: you could find tenants very quickly, the replacement would be guaranteed in a very short time. Last but not least, the purchase of a box provides for a lower initial expenditure than that of an apartment: this means that, by renting it, you would be more quickly covered in expenses incurred.

4. **Always look for the right deal and not the right property**

Many investors in real estate investments are influenced by their feelings. A property is not money. You can see it, touch it, you can like it or not and all this affects our taste, our feelings precisely, going to compromise what our brain would say instead. To be able to be objective we must detach from the building and we must focus on our real goal, the deal. We must estrange from the property itself and look at all the economic aspects (cost, estimated costs of maintenance, condominium costs, classification value and cadastral income that affect taxes, commercial compatibility of the property and the area in which it is located in its market), it is clear that a beautiful property in a beautiful area can affect our senses more than a sad apartment in a suburban area, but often in suburban residential areas can be obtained at low costs, excellent profits and continuity. Sometimes we strive to be objective but when we fall in love with something that objectivity fails without us even realizing it, it is at this moment that the role of our real estate consultant (that brings us back to the reality of the business, making us awaken from that 'falling in love) can be decisive preventing us from making a mistake that could cost us a bad deal.

5. **The income from a building must be seen in the continuity of the long term**

Sometimes when assessing the profitability of a property you look only at the maximum peak that the property can make without taking into account the time needed to make that property profitable.

Let's take a classic example, small property in a highly residential area of high value, clearly it is a building that can produce a high return and many dwell only on this without taking into account the fact that it is a property that can be used for short periods giving long breaks in which the income becomes a cost (tax, condominium), it is necessary time or costs (of real estate agencies) to get that income and can also be incurred more often than the maintenance costs in addition to risking more easily the problematic situations or arrears that, although kept under control

with the right tools, lead at least to an increase of time
to devote to the problem (if not incurred expenses or
lost revenue).

By following these advice, you can be sure that you will
get rich over time.

Chapter 9

Prepare for Retirement

If you want to retire early, the best way is to start using the power of compound interest. Here is what it is.

What is compound interest? Not everyone may know how to respond immediately to this question. In fact, if everyone knows what the simple interest is, i.e., the one that withdraws at the end of the agreed time unit, fewer are those who know what the compound interest is, how it works and, most importantly, how to take advantage of it.

The example of a bank account is enlightening.

If on 1 January I have a net rate of 1% on my account, at the end of the year I have 101 euros. The euro more is added to the capital and, if the conditions do not change, at the end of the second year I will not have 102 euros, but 102 euros and 1 cent where the cent represents 1% of the euro accumulated after the first year.

So far, everything is clear, but most of us cannot calculate the compound interest of an investment and tend to treat it as simple interest. This is due to its slow start, that, especially with small capital, tend to be treated as "irrelevant." However, there is nothing more wrong that an investor could do.

If, for example, after five years of investment, my capital of 100 euros is now 140, we are led to believe that the interest was 8% per year.

This is incorrect because, in doing so, we do not take into account that at the end of each period the interest accumulate has gone to increase capital. If the interest had really been 8%, composing the five years, we would have had

Initial capital: 100
- 1st year: 108

- 2nd year: 116.64
- 3rd year: 125.97
- 4th year: 136.04
- 5th year: 146.93

The difference (6.93 euros) represents almost 7% of the total. As you can see, it is easy to take dazzle (and worse, even "suffer," if for some reason we are offered a simple interest for a compound interest).

The maths behind compound interest: an easy example

Suppose we have an initial capital of 1,000 euros. The capital yields a Y% interest and this interest is calculated on an annual basis.

What will be the value of the investment after X years?

The calculation formula is as follows:

$$(1)\ IV = CP\ (1 + Y) \char`^ X$$

IV is the value of the investment after X years, while CP is the initial capital. Y is expressed as a percentage, i.e. 0.04 indicates 4%. The symbol ^ is the symbol of elevation to power.

The inverse calculation tends to find the Y interest of an investment that now (net of inflation) is worth IV against a CP capital invested X periods (years) ago. The formula is:

(2) Y = (IV / CP) ^ (1 / X) - 1

Suppose that, after inflation, 1,000 euros invested five years ago are now worth 1,400 euros, you immediately have that the yield was 6.96%.

Let's take a look at another example
Marie has just taken the salary and can finally buy the air conditioner she needs.

But her friend Julie calls her to tell her that she has an urgent need that she can not cope with immediately and asks her to borrow € 1,000.

Marie is undecided because this would mean waiting another month before she can make her purchase.

To resolve the issue, the two girls agree on the loan provided that Julie returns the money to Mary with a 5% interest (the numbers are purely random for the example).

In this way, Marie has a greater incentive to have to delay her purchase.

When Julie returns the sum loaned, she will receive € 1,050 instead of € 1,000.

The following month Marie can then buy the air conditioner and, to celebrate, use the € 50 interest to go out to dinner with her boyfriend.

In short, in the end, this recognition for the delayed use was not bad!

Now that we understand the concept behind the rate of interest it is good to enter a little more in detail and make some distinctions.

In this regard, we can divide the interest rate into two broad categories:

- The simple interest;
- The compound interests.

Simple Interest

Let's go back to the previous example.

At the end of the period, Julie returns the money plus the interest to Mary. Soon after, however, the girl asks again the same amount to buy a new refrigerator, as the old one suddenly broke.

Marie agrees to lend the money back to her friend.

The following month Julie firmed up her debt plus new interests, again for a total of € 1,050.

Now Marie is with her initial capital, plus € 100 in interest, for a total of € 1,100.

Interest is defined as simple when, once it has matured on the underlying capital, it does not generate further interest.

In our example, we note that the first 50 € was not added to the capital loaned the second time.

Compound Interest

Change of scenery.

Julie asks Marie to lend her € 1,000 with the promise to return them in two years.

Mary agrees, as long as Julie accepts a compound interest on the mature borrowed capital.

In this case, Julie will not have to pay the interest immediately at the end of the 1st year but will add the € 50 interest in the capital, which in turn will accumulate 5% in the 2nd year.

At the end of the agreed period, Julie must therefore return:

- € 1,000 capital
- € 50 interest for the first year (€ 1,000 + 5%)
- € 52.50 interest for the 2nd year (€ 1.050 + 5%)

The total capital to be returned to Mary is, therefore, € 1,102.50.

Here we have materialized € 2.50 more than the previous example, due to the compound interest.

The interest is defined as compound when, once it has matured on the underlying capital, it is added to the latter and contributes to generating further increased interest in the future.

Do you understand why the compound interest is your new best friend?

When you deposit your money in the bank account you are doing as Marie, that is, you are "lending" your money to the bank, which uses them to perform its credit function and lend it to people and businesses.
As a reward for this service, you are given an interest in the sums deposited, that is, a reward for the fact that you delay their use.

How to take advantage of the compound interest

If you do not want inflation to eat a nice slice of the real value and the purchasing power of your money, you have to make sure that the latter accrue compound interest over time.

Certainly, a part of the liquidity at your disposal you can deposit on one or more deposit accounts, or accounts with limited operations, where however higher interest rates are recognized.

For example, you could deposit your emergency fund.

The rest, however, you should invest in a portfolio of efficient financial instruments that protect your capital and create added value.

The compound interest must, therefore, be exploited for at least two reasons:

- Increase savings while waiting for their use;
- Defense against inflation.

A wise thing to do is, therefore, exploit the power of compound interest to make the value of your money grow faster, protecting it from loss of purchasing power.
Try to keep only small amounts on bank accounts that give you little to nothing.
You can leave just the right liquidity for your daily expenses and the emergency fund.

Are you looking for safe and profitable investments? Finding solutions of this type is not easy, you know very well, and that's why you decided to take the smartphone, the PC or the tablet to deepen.

In this chapter, we have decided to provide you with three concrete solutions to invest immediately, without making endless queues in the bank and without losing control of what you do.

The strategies that we suggest are ordered according to the risk profile, so we start from the less risky ones to get to the more aggressive ones.

We have written it in several books of this series; we underline it here too for safety: there are no safe investments and at the same time with double-digit returns. The times of government bonds and generous postal coupons have long since come to a close; the current economic situation sees interest at historic lows owing to the ECB's manoeuvrers in recent years.

In summary:

Few risks = Few Earnings
Many Risks = Potentially Increased Earnings but High Chances for Huge Losses

We come now to the merit of our discussion, here are

the best solutions for investing that we have chosen for you.

1. Santander Consumer Bank is the most remunerative deposit account

Are you looking for 100% capital guarantee? The deposit account is the best solution even if, in light of the considerations made before, you do not have to expect double-digit returns.

The best deposit account of the moment is that of Santander Consumer Bank which offers you an annual 1.8% on deposits at 36 months.

The advantages of Santander's offer can be summarized as follows:

- 100% security;
- Open it online: no stress, if you are from a PC, you need to fill out a form (you can do the same thing if you are on a smartphone) and just leave a few data. The procedure will be completed by phone at the time you indicated;
- No penalty in case of early release: if you

withdraw money before the scheduled time, you lose nothing;

- o Opening costs and management fees: you do not have to pay anything to make money.

To all this, we must add that Santander also provides the unconstrained option that allows you to receive 0.5% per year on free sums. This option can be mixed with the tied one: for example, out of 30 thousand euros, 20 thousand can be tied up at an interest rate of 1.8%, while the remaining 10 thousand free ones receive 0.5%.

Santander is a solid institution, active throughout the world with 122 million customers and over 160 years of history and is now the best solution for those looking for a deposit account free of risks and concerns.

2. MoneyFarm: the tech alternative to deposit accounts

Moneyfarm is an Italian startup that has created a convenient platform to invest online: it is easy to understand, and it is safe, we have also explained it in our review.

You can earn up to 5.41%.
The bank deposit accounts, at this stage, have returns that only in a few cases exceed 1.5%. If you're looking for granitic safety, go back to paragraph 1 where we talk about Santander.

However, if you are looking for better profitability at the same risk, you should pay attention to what you are reading. MoneyFarm, in fact, is an alternative to deposit accounts because it offers balanced investments with an almost similar degree of risk.

By signing up for MoneyFarm, you have the following advantages:

- Personal assistance of a team of competent advisors;
- Choose where to invest by filling in the questionnaire in which you indicate your degree of risk;
- You can start testing the goodness of the platform even with a small capital: just € 500 is

enough to try.

With MoneyFarm you can plan your investments and earn up to 5.41% per year, choosing the composition of your portfolio based on your risk profile.
Moneyfarm aims to invest in funds with lower operating costs and to guarantee maximum transparency to customers.
You can start investing immediately, even with € 500. Before choosing the strategy, the team of experts helps you to plan your goals exactly.

Registration is free: it takes 3 minutes to start to know it, you can also try it on a smartphone as it is really very easy to use.
Unlike many structured platforms for high-risk investments (think of trading or options), Moneyfarm allows you to operate even if you have a low-risk appetite and is undoubtedly a real alternative to deposit accounts or other banking products that make a lot less.

The portfolios are constantly monitored by a team of experts, and free assistance is guaranteed for the entire duration of the relationship.

It is possible to use the live chat service or to set up a telephone appointment thanks to a special toll-free number. The seriousness is certified by the prizes and awards obtained by leading international financial experts and opinions on the web that are positive. You also choose how much you are willing to risk, and the staff helps you plan the route step by step.

3. Social Trading

Compared to the previous solution, we are facing a decidedly riskier way: let's underline it immediately, to avoid misunderstandings. If the world of finance interests you, keep reading carefully because you found what you were looking for.

Have you ever tried to approach online trading? If you did and you gave up, most likely you came across the difficulties of a world where only the professional traders, that is, have experience, years of study and time to constantly monitor what is going on. Happening in the market in which they operate.

The social trading, we want to talk about is precisely

created to solve this gap in skills between professional and non-professional investors. eToro, the first social trading platform, allows you to make copy trading: you can, in other words, copy the winning strategies of top traders emulating their successes.

The principle is simple: by investing as the best, you earn like the best.

Chapter 10

Holding Some Investments Forever

Buying and holding forever is one of the best ways to get rich. However, because of the continuous ups and downs that have involved international stock exchanges in recent months, many have begun to ask themselves the fateful question: "Is investing in stocks still the best strategy to multiply my savings?".

The financial markets, in general, can be an extraordinary opportunity: not only stocks but also cryptocurrencies or forex can give great satisfaction even if, however, it is necessary to have preparation before going into rash choices.

In this chapter, we will go deep into the subject and discover the 17 golden lessons that every investor should know, before entering the stock market.

1. **Easy money is like Santa Claus: it does not exist!**

Who promises to quintuple your assets without sweating is not more than a seller of smoke: investing in the stock market is not a joke and to achieve the investment goals you have set yourself to avoid risky securities, focusing on something more stable, lasting and profitable. In the recipe for success, in addition to a serious knowledge of the stock markets, there is also the sentimental component (for those investing there is no room for panic but a lot of patience) and even a bit of luck.

2. Gold and cash do not give interest

Everyone knows that cash does not disappear, but after the bizarre manoeuvrers of the European Central Bank (which brought negative returns on the single currency), we can be even more certain that investing in cash does not create any interest. The dream of all is to be able to accumulate that amount of money enough to enjoy a quiet retirement but the closer it gets to the time x, the more the small investor tends to panic. Hence the reckless choices to invest in cash or in commodities such as gold which, although it proves to be more stable than fiat, cannot hold the same value forever. Just think that in the last luster, the value of the most precious metal fell by 34.8%.

3. The ingredients for a winning strategy

One of the main factors of success on the stock exchange is sentiment: patience, foresight, and prudence are the three basic ingredients of winning strategies, but it is also true that a little risk never hurts.

If the money we have invested on a certain stock does not return, you should look around and find some slightly riskier but at least profitable activity, with the hope that an important injection of money into the markets can restart the economy by stimulating productivity and development.

4. Establish investment goals

Before starting to invest, then embark on a challenging and long path, you must have clear in mind where you want to go. It depends on personal aspirations, on the trust that one has for himself and on many other factors. However, the main choice is between protecting capital and making it grow. Under certain conditions, the stock exchange also lends itself to the speculative approach. Who wants to start could also establish concrete objectives such as buying a good or a service. In any case, the rule is always the same: to understand where you want to arrive.

5. Establish the degree of risk tolerance

This is probably the most important phase. The stock market is in fact extremely varied and allows numerous approaches, from the prudent and static to the dynamic and courageous.

This is why it is always good to establish one's degree of tolerance. Based on this decision, further choices will be made, until the real investment is realized. Investor profiles depend on personal characteristics and their economic situation. If you are a simple worker, do not sail in gold and maybe those who invest are the savings of a lifetime, it is good to give up any speculative ambitions. The degree of tolerance determines the risk that you intend to run and the strategy that will be adopted later.

6. Studying

The information issue should not be forgotten. The stock market is complex, structurally risky, so we need to be cautious. The risk is to lose capital in a short period. Therefore, it is necessary to undertake a training course that confers at least the theoretical tools. The topic of the study should consist of both the investment modalities - how it is invested in the concrete - and the economic environment in general.
As for the sources, including paper texts, successful books, and the internet, you are spoiled with choices.
The study activity, however, never abandons the investor, even when he has become an expert. Pressing is the need to update continuously, but also to inquire about everything that gravitates around the securities in the portfolio.

7. Choose the long-term

Investing in the stock market should not be an act of a few months or even a few years. It must be a continuous activity. It is only through patience and perseverance that it is possible to make substantial profits. This means that you need to build a long-term version, which looks at least for the next five years (even if ten are more suitable). This means that it is good not to give in to the temptation to sell the securities as soon as the prices start to fall. In the bag as in life is worth the saying "laugh well who laughs last."

8. Monitoring

If you opt for a long-term vision, as you should, then it is essential to monitor the status of your investment. Not everyone knows that control and monitoring begin before the investment itself. In particular, it is necessary to establish a benchmark, i.e., a yardstick by means of which it is possible to really understand whether we are on the right path or not. Finally, it is good to make a periodic comparison between the expected results and the real ones. In the beginning, there is a strong temptation to abandon oneself to discouragement, also because the results tend to arrive farther with time.

A general consideration can be made on the segment within which to operate. In fact, everything depends on risk tolerance. If this is very low, you should address those segments that by their nature do not suffer from the crisis. The reference is to those goods whose consumption is practically mandatory, therefore the food and pharmaceuticals. Investing in pharmaceutical companies' actions will not make you rich but is a very useful asset to protect capital. Strangely enough, but up to a certain point, the high-tech segment (e.g., mobile phones, social networks, etc.) also plays a similar role.

Investing in the stock market can be a business that can increase its capital. In addition to technical knowledge, we need some moral skills: patience, perseverance, lucidity, foresight. All qualities that must be cultivated and that can make the difference. Vice versa will never give good fruits an approach based on imprudence, on haste, from the frenzy of profit.

9. Use the leverage

What unfortunately many traders do not consider is investing in the stock market or trading online using leverage. To invest in the stock market with little money, it is necessary to deepen the study of this tool, which will allow us to expose our capital to a huge risk.

We recommend the use of leverage only on a reduced capital, carried out concurrently also with a rationalized use of stop loss and take profit. In addition, you must always have your budget under control using careful Money Management. Finally, before investing in the stock market, you need to study the markets and all the financial instruments on which you want to invest in.

10. You do not need to be a finance guru to invest in the stock market!

Obviously, we are not telling you that the market should not be studied or that there must be a basis for training. Who applies himself and follows the markets, deepening the subject, will always know more than others.

So, we always recommend following the training path of your broker, which will allow you not to take missteps throughout the investment process. Taking advantage of the online trading demo platforms, it is possible to simulate the investment and understand where mistakes are made and avoid them when investing with a real account.

11. Use only trusty brokers

We believe that the stock market is not a market for everyone but for a few! Above all we can not recommend the stock exchange, the investments on the stock exchange to those subjects are not inclined to study at least basic and training. In this case, it is better to let go of one's own, as it is not possible to rely only on luck.

Our advice is to stay away if you do not have and do not want to learn specific skills. If you do not have a basic education, all the savings you invest will lose them in less than a month. On the contrary, instead, we recommend investing in the stock market with online trading and regulated brokers. This is because, being regulated and being subjected to strict controls, they do not put capital at risk and also the broker will provide you with a fair and complete formation. Below you will find a complete list of regulated and authorized brokers to invest with.

12. Learn technical analysis

Technical analysis is the study of price trends with the use of graphs. The interest of a technical analyst is to look for the graphic configurations that are drawn by price movements. The market trend is evaluated to understand possible future price movements.

The pure technical analysis is not based on any fundamental of the underlying activity but applies a series of technical tools drawn on the chart, in order to allow for future courses.

On the chart, price movements are usually represented by bars or candles, allowing price analysis in a certain period called 'timeframe.'

On a candle, the body or the central part represents the difference between opening and closing in a given period. The shadows, i.e. the top and bottom segments, represent the difference between the maximum and the minimum of the period considered and the opening or closing of the candle.

We can have monthly, daily, 1 hour, 5 minutes or even shorter candles.

The different colors of the candles indicate a rise or fall in the period. Usually, a green candle represents a rise in prices, which means that the closing price of the candle is higher than the opening one, while the red candle represents a drop.

The levels of the chart where prices find an obstacle are called 'levels of support or resistance.' A 'support' is the level at which a bearish price halts its downfall and potentially 'rebounds' up again. The most significant support is repeatedly tested and becomes the level of support from a technical point of view. The 'resistance' is the opposite of the support. It is the level at which a rising price finds an obstacle to rise further and instead shows a decline. Even a resistance tested several times takes on higher strategic importance.

When prices determine an important level of support but then violate it downwards, this level of support becomes an important area of resistance. The same goes for resistance that if violated on the upside turns into a significant level of support.

There are so many indicators used by technical analysts to try and predict the next price movements. One of the most used indicators is the 'simple moving average,' which is calculated on a certain amount of price data and is mobile because it moves from period to period.

Given an average of a certain time frame, the most recent data is added each time, eliminating the last data in the series from the calculation. The moving average can be used as a support or dynamic resistance. The most used periods on the daily chart for the moving average are 50, 100 and 200. If prices show an important uptrend, the moving average will be an important medium / short-term support, inversely if prices show a bearish trend the average mobile will be a significant dynamic resistance.

13. Learn fundamental analysis

Unlike the previous one, it is based on the study of the company and its reference market.

In practice, it is based on balance sheet data, on management's ability and credibility, on trends in the specific sector in which the company operates. In this case, one must also consider:

- value investing;
- growth investing;
- investment.

All traders have a different investing style. Every trader has his investment techniques, and each has his particular techniques, as well as his particular tricks and his particular "secrets."

But do not be fooled by the strange idea of being able to learn how to invest by reading articles on the internet. This is impossible. You can find excellent advice but not the magic formula. At most, you could clear your mind and give yourself a general orientation, but to get serious you need longer and more in-depth things.

14. Analyze the state of the market

Closely connected to the concept of technical analysis and fundamental analysis is the concept of analysis of the general market. It does not matter whether you are a professional investor or a beginner, this will be the most difficult step you need to understand.

In practice, it is pure art applied to scientific instruments. You must first understand and analyze the market for the sole purpose of formulating a plausible development scenario. This also means accumulating an enormous amount of data and statistics regarding the performance of the securities and developing the "sensitivity" necessary to choose the truly relevant ones.

If you put this into practice, you will also understand why many investors buy the shares of a particular company and not of another one.

At the same time, we always advise you to observe the products you have at home. Although this element may seem unusual, it is very important to understand that you have direct knowledge of many products and not others. In practice it will allow you to perform a quick and intuitive analysis of the financial performance of the manufacturing companies, comparing them with those of their competitors.

Before investing, you must reflect on the products examined; For example, try to imagine the economic conditions for which you might decide to stop buying them or increase or decrease your stocks. This is a great exercise to get a feeling of what an average person needs and treats as "important."

15. Create an investment plan

A very important step. You have to create an investment plan, but to do that you must first of all fully understand why you want to invest.

You must know how much you can invest in and how much you want to invest in achieving your goals. You must also have clear ideas about what your goals are.

To do this, you could always use an Excel sheet or even a special tool to calculate how much you will have to spend to achieve your goals.

Based on the income you can afford to invest then, calculate the type of investment. You can not claim to want to get € 10,000 from an investment if what you can afford to invest in trading online or on the stock exchange or even in other systems does not exceed 1000 euros. Everything must be proportionate. Start small and build it up over time.

16. Understand Asset Location

Defined as the distribution of liquidity in the various investment instruments available should vary depending on the stage of life in which you are.

This means that if you are young, the percentage of your investment portfolio relative to the shares will have to be higher. On the contrary, if you have a solid and well-paid career, your job is like an obligation! You can use it in order to guarantee long-term income. Here's all this allows you to allocate most of your financial portfolio in shares.

At the same time, you have to understand that if you have a job whose remuneration is not predictable, as in the case where you are self-employed, then you have to allocate most of your financial portfolio in more stable products; in this case, it is better to invest in bonds, perhaps government bonds and not in shares.

At the same time, however, you must consider that the actions allow faster growth of your invested assets but as such entails a greater risk.

Conclusion

Thanks for making it through to the end of this book, let's hope it was informative and able to provide you with all of the tools you need to achieve your financial goals.

The next step is to begin to apply what you have learned during the course of this book and get started right away. Remember that you should never risk more than what you can afford to lose, so manage your capital wisely.

We hope that you find these lessons valuable and that you got the information you were looking for. Letting your money work for you will give you an incredible feeling, especially at the beginning, when you make the first gains. We are thrilled for you to start and we cannot wait to see your results coming in.